Western Esotericism

SUNY series in Western Esoteric Traditions
———————
David Appelbaum, editor

Western Esotericism

A Concise History

Antoine Faivre

translated by
Christine Rhone

Originally published in French as *L'Ésotérisme*. © Presses Universitaires de France, 1992. 6. avenue Reille. 75014 Paris

Cover art: A picture by Dionysius Andreas Freher, in *The Works of Jacob Behmen, The Teutonic Philosopher*, edited by William Law, vol. 3, 1764. Private collection of the author.

Published by State University of New York Press, Albany

© 2010 State University of New York

For information, contact State University of New York Press, Albany, NY
www.sunypress.edu

Production by Eileen Meehan
Marketing by Anne M. Valentine   .

Library of Congress Cataloging-in-Publication Data

Faivre, Antoine, 1934–
    [Accès de l'ésotérisme occidental. English]
    Western esotericism : a concise history / Antoine Faivre ; Christine Rhone, translator.
        p. cm. — (Suny series in Western esoteric traditions)
    Includes bibliographical references and indexes.
    ISBN 978-1-4384-3377-6 (hardcover : alk. paper)
    ISBN 978-1-4384-3378-3 (pbk. : alk. paper)
    1. Occultism--History.   I. Rhone, Christine.   II. Title.

BF1412.F313 2010
135'.4—dc22   2010015998

10 9 8 7 6 5 4 3 2 1

Contents

Introduction

In 2010, historian Monika Neugebauer-Wölk showed that the noun esotericism occurs as early as 1792. In that year, it appeared in German: *Esoterik*,[1] in the context of debates concerning the secret teachings of Pythagoras against a background of Freemasonry. In a context with affinities to Romanticism, it first appeared in French in 1828 in *Histoire critique du Gnosticisme et de son influence* by Jacques Matter (as Jean-Pierre Laurant pointed out in 1992). The term has since revealed itself, in English and in other languages, as semantically expandable and permeable as one likes.

To question its etymology (*eso* refers to the idea of interiority, and *ter* evokes an opposition) is hardly productive and often stems from a need to discover what "esotericism" in "itself" would be (its "true" nature). In fact, there is no such thing, although those who claim the contrary are many—these individuals approaching it according to their own definitions, in function of their own interests or ideological presuppositions. It seems more productive to us to begin by inventorying the various meanings that it takes according to the speakers.

I. Five Meanings of the Word *Esotericism*

1. Meaning 1: A Disparate Grouping

In this meaning, which is the most current, esotericism appears, for example, as the title of sections in bookshops and in much media

---

1. About that first know occurrence, see Monika Neugebauer-Wölk's ground-breaking article (in *Aries* 10:1, 2010). As she explains, that term *Esoterik* was from the pen of Johann Philipp Gabler, who used it in his edition of Johann Gottfried Eichhorn's *Urgeschichte* (1792).

discourse to refer to almost everything that exudes a scent of mystery. Oriental wisdom traditions, yoga, mysterious Egypt, ufology, astrology and all sorts of divinatory arts, parapsychology, various "Kabbalahs," alchemy, practical magic, Freemasonry, Tarot, New Age, New Religious Movements, and channeling are found thus placed side by side (in English, the label used in the bookshops is often *Occult* or *Metaphysics*). This nebula often includes all sorts of images, themes, and motifs, such as ontological androgyny, the Philosopher's Stone, the lost Word, the Soul of the World, sacred geography, the magic book, and so on.

2. Meaning 2: Teachings or Facts That Are "Secret" Because They Are Deliberately Hidden

This is for example the "discipline of the arcane," the strict distinction between the initiated and the profane. Thus, "esoteric" often is employed as a synonym of "initiatic," including by certain historians treating doctrines that would have been kept secret, for example, among the first Christians. For the wider public, it also refers to the idea that secrets would have been jealously guarded during the course of centuries by the church magisterium, such as the secret life of Christ, his close relationship with Mary Magdalene—or that important messages would have been surreptitiously slipped into a work by their author. Novels like the parodical *Il Pendolo di Foucault* (1988) by Umberto Eco and the mystery-mongering *The Da Vinci Code* (2003) by Dan Brown skillfully take advantage of the taste of a broad audience for what belongs to the so-called "conspiracy theories."

3. Meaning 3: A Mystery Is Inherent in Things Themselves

Nature would be full of occult "signatures"; there would exist invisible relationships between stars, metals, and plants; human History would also be "secret," not because people would have wanted to hide certain events, but because it would contain meanings to which the "profane" historian would not have access. *Occult philosophy*, a term widely used in the Renaissance, is in its diverse forms an endeavor to decipher such mysteries. Similarly, some call the "hidden God" the "esoteric God" (the one not entirely revealed.)

4. Meaning 4: "Gnosis," Understood as a Mode of Knowledge Emphasizing the "Experiential," the Mythical, the Symbolic, Rather Than Forms of Expression of a Dogmatic and Discursive Order

The ways enabling one to gain this "way of knowledge" vary according to the schools; it is the subject of initiatic teachings given forth in groups claiming to possess it, but sometimes it is also considered as accessible without them. Understood in this way, esotericism often is associated with the notion of "religious marginality" for those who intend to make a distinction between the various forms of gnosis, and the established traditions or the constituted religions.

5. Meaning 5: The Quest for the "Primordial Tradition"

The existence of a "primordial Tradition" is posited, of which the various traditions and religions spread throughout the world would be only fragmented and more or less "authentic" pieces. Here, esotericism is the teaching of the ways that would permit attaining knowledge of this Tradition or contributing to restore it. Nowadays, this teaching is principally that of the "Traditionalist School," also known as "perennialism" (chapter 5, section II), whose English-speaking representatives readily use the word *esoterism* to distinguish themselves from most of the other meanings of esotericism.

Despite certain relationships of proximity, these five meanings evidently differ from one another. It is a matter of knowing which one we are dealing with when someone employs this "portmanteau word" (the same goes for other words, such as "religion," "sacred," "magic," "spirituality," "mysticism," etc.). Taken in the first sense, it can refer to almost anything. Let us take the example of "mysterious Egypt"; still today, many authors take pleasure in uncovering an "esotericism" in ancient Egypt present in the form of initiations and sublime knowledge. Yet these practices scarcely existed in Ancient Egypt, except in their own modern *imaginaire*[2]; and even supposing

---

2. In this context, *imaginaire* does not mean "belief in things that are false or unreal" but refers to the "representations" that consciously or unconsciously underlie and/or permeate a discourse, a conversation, a literary or artistic work, a current of thought, a political or philosophical trend, and so forth. Thus understood, this term is sometimes translated as "the imaginary" or "the imaginary world" (German: *Weltbild*), but in the present book we keep the original French [Translator's note].

that they are partly right (which it is permitted to doubt), it would never be a matter there of more than a form of religiosity present in many religious systems, which it would be sufficient to call, for example, "sacred mysteries." It is no less legitimate and interesting, for the historian, to study the various forms of egyptomania proper to the Western esoteric currents because they are often part of their thematic repertory. Furthermore, through intellectual laziness, people often use the term *esoteric* to qualify particular images, themes, or motifs that they readily lump together under the heading "esoteric" (cf. *infra*, section I on the "unicorn" and similar notions).

The second sense encompasses both too much and too little (besides the fact that, when there are secrets, they are generally open ones). It includes too much, because the idea of "deliberately hidden things" is universal. It includes too little, because it would be false to call "secrets" a number of currents or traditions, as for example—to limit ourselves to the period from the fifteenth to the seventeenth century—alchemy, neo-Alexandrian Hermetism, theosophy, Rosicrucianism. In fact, for its greater part, alchemy (both material and "spiritual") is not secret because it has never ceased to make itself known through abundant publications supplied to a wide public. Renaissance Hermetism (see *infra*, section II) is never more than one of the manifestations of the humanist current, which addressed all the literate. The theosophical writings have always circulated in the most varied milieux, Christian and other. Rosicrucianism of the seventeenth century is mostly a sort of politico-religious program.

The idea according to which the "real" would be in great part "hidden" by its very nature—third meaning—is present in all cultures, and, as it assumes various connotations in them, it is preferable to find a more precise term to define each one of them. Similarly, concerning the fourth meaning—"esotericism" as a synonym of "gnosis"—it can seem pointless to complicate matters by not remaining content with this second word. Certainly, a number of those who intend to speak of "esotericism in itself" attempt to find equivalent terms in cultures distinct from ours (in India, in the Far East, etc.); but the point is not convincing because the terms thus employed do not possess the same semantic charge and refer to very different meanings. The fifth meaning, finally, also designates something relatively precise (a rather specific current of thought); at that point, it would be enough for the exterior observer to employ the term *perennialism* rather than esotericism (although those connected with this current have, of course, the right to use the second term). Notwithstanding, and as we have seen, they themselves prefer, in English, to speak of esoterism rather than esotericism.

For these various reasons, esotericism is understood (especially since about the beginning of the 1990s; cf. *infra*, sections II, IV, and V) in a sixth meaning for the majority of historians.

II. Sixth Meaning:
A Group of Specific Historical Currents

Indeed, these historians, as we did in our first works on the notion of esotericism at the beginning of the 1990s (*infra*, section IV), have preserved the word through sheer convenience (it had the merit of already existing) to refer to the "history of Western esoteric currents." These currents, as we shall see, present strong similarities and are found to have historical interconnections.

Western here refers to a West—a West permeated by Christian culture and "visited" by Jewish or Muslim religious traditions, or even Far Eastern ones, with which it cohabited but that are not identical with it; in this understanding, Jewish Kabbalah does not belong to this "Western esotericism," whereas the so-called Christian Kabbalah does. Of course, this choice, which is purely methodological, does not imply any judgmental position whatsoever.

Among the currents that illustrate this "Western esotericism" (in the sixth meaning) appear notably, for late Antiquity and the Middle Ages, the following ones: Alexandrian Hermetism (the Greek writings attributed to the legendary Hermes Trismegistus, second and third centuries of our era); Christian Gnosticism, various forms of neo-Pythagoreanism, speculative astrology, and alchemy. And for the so-called modern period, let us cite especially, in the Renaissance, neo-Alexandrian Hermetism, Christian Kabbalah (corpus of interpretations of Jewish Kabbalah intending to harmonize it with Christianity), the *philosophia occulta*, the so-called Paracelsian current (from the name of the philosopher Paracelsus), and some of its derivatives. After the

Renaissance, we have Rosicrucianism and its variants, as well as Christian theosophy, the "Illuminism" of the eighteenth century, a part of romantic *Naturphilosophie*, the so-called "occultist" current (from the mid-nineteenth century to the beginning of the twentieth). According to some representatives of this specialty, "Western esotericism" extends over this vast field, from late Antiquity to the present (broad meaning). According to other representatives of this same specialty, it is preferable to understand it in a more restricted sense by limiting it to the so-called "modern" period (from the Renaissance until today); they then speak of a "modern Western esotericism" (restricted meaning).

This short book follows the second approach (restricted meaning), although the first chapter deals with the ancient and medieval sources of the modern Western esoteric currents, that is to say, the first fifteen centuries of our era. The reason for this choice is that starting from the end of the fifteenth century new currents appeared, in a very innovative fashion in the sense that they found themselves intrinsically connected with nascent modernity, to the point of constituting a specific product. They in fact reappropriated, in a Christian light but in original ways, elements having belonged to late Antiquity and to the Middle Ages (such as Stoicism, Gnosticism, Hermetism, neo-Pythagoreanism). Indeed, only at the beginning of the Renaissance did people begin to want to collect a variety of antique and medieval materials of the type that concerns us, in the belief that they could constitute a homogenous group. Marsilio Ficino, Pico della Mirandola, and others (chapter 2, section I) undertook to consider them as mutually complementary, to seek their common denominators, as far as postulating the existence of a *philosophia perennis* (a "perennial philosophy"). Real or mythical, the representatives of the latter were considered the links in a chain illustrated by Moses, Zoroaster, Hermes Trismegistus, Plato, Orpheus, the Sibyls, and sometimes also by other characters. Thus, for example, after the expulsion of the Jews from Spain in 1492, Jewish Kabbalah penetrated into the Christian milieu to find itself interpreted in the light of traditions (Alexandrian Hermetism, alchemy, Pythagoreanism, etc.) that were not Jewish.

Reasons of a theological order account, largely, for such a need to have recourse to ancient traditions. For a long time, indeed, Christianity had preserved within it certain forms of "knowledge" that entered into the field of theology (or theologies) and related to the connection between metaphysical principles and cosmology (the Aristotelian "second causes"). But after theology had, little by little, discarded cosmology, that is to say, part of itself, then this vast field found itself appropriated, reinterpreted "from the outside" (outside the theological field) by an extra-theological attempt to connect the universal to the particular—to occupy the interface between metaphysics and cosmology. Many thinkers of the Renaissance tried to justify such an attempt by resorting to certain traditions of the past.

To that attempt is added, as a corollary, the idea of "revelations possible from within Revelation itself" (to employ the felicitous expression suggested by the historian Jean-Pierre Brach). In other terms, believers who adhered to the teaching of their Church could nevertheless benefit from a "revelation" not dispensed by the official catechism ("Revelation" as it is taught), but which by its very nature would be consistent with deepening the meaning and the content of this catechism. Those who exploited the certitude of this "inner revelation" tended rather to impersonal discourse, either by exhibiting a tradition to which they would have had access, a transmission of which they would be the repositories, or by affirming themselves graced with an inspiration come directly from on high. This idea is very present, certainly, in the three great religions of the Book (where it often finds itself challenged by the existing orthodoxies), but in the Renaissance era it is also a means of enriching an official teaching felt as impoverished—and it would remain very present in the history of modern esoteric currents.

Finally, these three areas of discourse (the search for a perennial philosophy, the autonomization of an extra-theological discourse in the subject of cosmology, and the idea of possible revelation from within Revelation) constitute, particularly the first two, an essential aspect of nascent modernity. For the latter, which then finds itself confronted with itself, it is a matter of answering questions posed by its own advent—and not, as is too often believed, the response of a sort of "counter-culture" directed against modernity. This remark is just as applicable, as we shall see, to the subsequent esoteric currents.

III. From the Religionist and Universalist Approach to the Historico-Critical Approach

To treat esotericism understood in this sixth sense (*supra*, section II) comes within a historico-critical mode of approach. We will return (*infra*, sections IV, V) to the ways in which it is declined; but, before that, it seems necessary to introduce another one, followed by many authors who also intend to treat the history of "esotericism." This introduction will permit us, at the same time, to bring out some of the implications with which meanings one to five are charged.

This second mode of approach rests either on a "religionist" position, or on a "universalist" position, or again on both at the same time. The first consists in positing that, to validly study a religion, a tradition, a spiritual trend, and so on—and, consequently, "esotericism"—it is necessary to be a member of it oneself on pain of not understanding very much about it—hence the proselytizing tendency frequently evinced by the supporters of this position. The second consists in postulating the existence of a "universal esotericism" of which it would be a matter of discovering, of explicating the "true" nature; we can remark that, in this type of discourse, esotericism is most of the time synonymous with "sacred" in general, indeed of "religion" understood *sub specie aeternitatis*.

The simultaneously religionist and universalist position is represented principally by the perennialist current evoked in section I, which spread in most of the Western countries especially from the mid-twentieth century. It will be (chapter 5, section II) the subject of a specific discussion. The following are two examples of scholarly religionists. In France, Robert Amadou, whose work is abundant; his first significant work is entitled *L'occultisme. Esquisse d'un monde vivant* (1950). "Occultism" is here synonymous with "esotericism" understood in the second, third, and fourth meanings at once; despite his somewhat universalizing bent, Amadou distinguishes himself strongly, let us note, from perennialism (fifth meaning). In Germany, Gerhard Wehr, who limits his field to the Western world and attempts, throughout a series of high-quality monographs, to find concordances between Rudolf Steiner, Carl Gustav Jung, Novalis, Jacob Boehme, and the like, and who occasionally paints a picture of what is according to him Christian esotericism (*Esoterisches Christentum*, 1975 and 1995). An example of a universalist is the academic Pierre Riffard, who has posited (in *L'ésotérisme: Qu'est-ce que l'ésotérisme? Anthologie de l'ésotérisme*, 1990) the existence of a "universal esotericism" composed, according to him, of eight invariables:

1. The impersonality of the authors;
2. The opposition between the profane and the initiates;
3. The subtle;
4. Correspondences;
5. Numbers;
6. The occult sciences;
7. The occult arts; and
8. Initiation.

Although admitting that this construction could lend itself to an inquiry of an anthropological and/or philosophical type, it would not be of much use to the historian.

In the intellectual climate of the 1960s and 1970s, scholarly philosophers and historians tended to see in the esoteric currents (as well as in various forms of "spirituality") of the past a sort of "counter-culture" that would have been generally beneficial to humanity and from which it would be in the best interests of our disenchanted era to learn. Belonging to this movement are a certain number of personalities connected with the Eranos group, such as Carl Gustav Jung, Mircea Eliade, Henry Corbin, Ernst Benz, Gilbert Durand, or Joseph Campbell. Certainly, the Eranos Conferences held at Anscona (Switzerland) from 1933 to 1984, of which all the Proceedings have been published, have contributed to stimulate the interest of a good part of the academic world, as much for comparativism in the history of religions as for various forms of esotericism. However, because of their mainly apologetic orientation, they have not failed to give rise to reservations on the part of researchers of a more strictly historical orientation, notably of those whose works bear on esotericism understood in the sixth sense of the term. This is also the period when Frances A. Yates (*infra*) described the Renaissance magus as a rebel opposed to the dogmas of the established Churches and, later, to the pretentions of mechanistic science (although Yate's purpose was not apologetic in character).

Among the historians of esotericism understood in the sixth sense, it is appropriate to distinguish two categories. On the one hand, those who, very numerous, work on currents (movements, societies) or particular authors; their aim is not (which is certainly their right) to question the existence or the nature of the considered specialty as such; this is discussed in chapter 5, section II. And, on the other hand, the "generalists," who intend to study "esotericism" as a whole (of course, "universalists" like Riffard are in their manner generalists, but here we consider only those who adopt a historico-critical approach). They study it considering it either *lato sensu*, or *stricto sensu* (the twenty centuries of our era, or only the so-called "modern" period, which begins at the Renaissance; cf. section II). Most of the "generalists" adopt (following the example of the "nongeneralists") an empirical approach of a historico-critical type; at that point, it is not surprising that they prove to have a real methodological concern. In any event, they intend to distinguish themselves from the many works of a religionist character, including those whose importance they nevertheless recognize at least with regard to the "origins" of their specialty—thus, it is undeniable that the Eranos Conferences (cf. *supra*), for example, have contributed to stimulate the interest of the academic world in this same specialty.

The book (of a nonreligionist and nonuniversalist orientation) of Frances Yates, *Giordano Bruno and the Hermetic Tradition*, published in 1964, prepared the way for the academic recognition of this field of study understood in the sixth sense. With respect to this work, it has been possible to speak of a "Yates paradigm," which rests on two ideas: a) there would have existed from the fifteenth to the seventeenth century a "Hermetic tradition" opposing the dominant traditions of Christianity and rationality; b) it would have paradoxically constituted an important positive factor in the development of the scientific revolution. These two propositions are debatable, but the *Giordano Bruno* has nonetheless stimulated the lively interest of many researchers in this notion of the "Hermetic tradition" applied not only to the period of the Renaissance (studied by Yates), but also to those that followed it and that preceded it. In fact, her "paradigm" found itself supplanted by another, introduced by the author of these lines (in 1992 notably, in the first edition of this little book; cf. *infra*, section IV).

IV. A New Manner of Constructing the Object

In examining the possibility of founding a new paradigm, we decided from the outset to differentiate ourselves from what "esotericists" or their adversaries, and even from what historians however not ideologically engaged, could have understood by "esotericism" (or, like Yates, "Hermetic tradition"). In fact, most of them have the tendency thus to refer to an "ideal type" (other examples of ideal types: "reason," "faith," "sacred," "magic," "gnosis," "mysticism," etc.), which they adopt at first as an *a priori* and to which they strive, in a second phase, to make particular phenomena correspond. Therefore, it was not a matter of constructing or reconstructing a hypothetical "esoteric doctrine," for example, but of beginning by observing empirically (without an essentialist or apologetic presupposition) a dense series of varied materials taken in a historical period and a geographical area (the modern period in the West). It was then a matter of asking ourselves if some of these materials would have sufficient common characteristics (hence, in the plural) so that, as a whole, they could be considered a specific field. For this to have been, it seemed essential to us that there should be several characteristics—a single one would have ineluctably conferred a universal scope on the constructed object, which it was precisely a matter of avoiding.

In fact, a certain number of characteristics emerged from this observation. Taken as a whole, they constitute a construct (a working model)—that of the object "Modern Western Esotericism" (as it has been called at our suggestion). This object would be identifiable by the simultaneous presence of a certain number of components distributed according to variable proportions (in a text, in an author, in a trend, even though obviously a discourse is never only "esoteric"). Four are intrinsic (fundamental), in the sense that their simultaneous presence suffices to identify the object. Two others are "secondary," in the sense that they appear only frequently, but they nonetheless confer a greater flexibility on this construct.

The four fundamental characteristics are as follows:

1. *The idea of universal correspondences.* Non-"causal" correspondences operate between all the levels of reality of the universe, which is a sort of theater of mirrors inhabited and animated by invisible forces. For example, there would exist relationships between the heavens (macrocosm) and the human being (microcosm), between the planets and the parts of the human body, between the revealed texts of religions (the Bible, principally) and what Nature shows us, between these texts and the History of humanity.

2. *The idea of living Nature.* The cosmos is not only a series of correspondences. Permeated with invisible but active forces, the whole of Nature, considered as a living organism, as a person, has a history, connected with that of the human being and of the divine world. To that are often added interpretations, heavy with implications, of the passage from Romans 7:19–22 according to which suffering Nature, subject to the exile and to vanity, also awaits its deliverance.

3. *The role of mediations and of the imagination.* These two notions are mutually complementary. Rituals, symbols charged with multiple meanings (mandala, Tarot cards, biblical verse, etc.), and intermediary spirits (hence, angels) appear as so many mediations. These have the capacity to provide passages between different levels of reality, when the "active" imagination (the "creative" or "magical" imagination—a specific, but generally dormant faculty of the human mind), exercised on these mediations, makes them a tool of knowledge (*gnosis*), indeed, of "magical action on the real."

4. *The experience of transmutation.* This characteristic comes to complete the three preceding ones by conferring an "experiential" character on them. It is the transformation of oneself, which can be a "second birth"; and as a corollary that of a part of Nature (e.g., in a number of alchemical texts).

As far as the two so-called secondary characteristics are concerned, they are, on the one hand, a practice of *concordance*: It is a matter of positing *a priori* that common denominators can exist among several different traditions, indeed among all of them, and then of undertaking to compare them with a view to finding a higher truth that overhangs them. And it is, on the other hand, the emphasis put on the idea of *transmission*: Widespread in these esoteric currents especially since the eighteenth century, it consists in insisting on the importance of "channels of transmission"; for example, "transmission" from master to disciple, from the initiator to the "initiable" (self-initiation is not possible). To be valuable or valid, this transmission is often considered necessarily to belong to an affiliation whose authenticity ("regularity") is considered genuine. This aspect concerns the Western esoteric currents especially starting at the time when they began to give birth to initiatic societies (i.e., starting from the mid-eighteenth century).

This model amounted, in fact, to constructing the very object of a specialty for which no theoretical construct (at least, of an empirico-critical character) had yet been proposed. It often has been employed by other researchers, even though, like any working model, it has been the object of some criticism relative to some of its implications. As Wouter J. Hanegraaff, for example, has remarked, it would not sufficiently account for the importance of movements like the pietism of the seventeenth century, or for the process of secularization undergone by the esoteric currents of the nineteenth and the twentieth. Anyhow, it is an acknowledged fact that no construct should be considered as a "truth" by its proponent; actually, it is nothing but a provisional heuristic tool meant to revive fresh methodological thinking. To wit, a number of scholars have contributed, subsequently, to refine our working tool (*infra*, section V).

It seemed to us that the expression "form of thought" (however debatable the choice of this expression may be) could be applied to this modern Western esotericism thus defined. Perhaps it could be claimed—which is not our purpose—that it appears in other cultures or periods as well. Still it would be appropriate to confine ourselves to the empirical observation of the facts; that is, not to hypostatize this expression with a view to legitimating the idea according to which there would exist a sort of "universal esotericism." Just as there is a form of thought of an esoteric type, so there exist forms of thought of a scientific, mystical, theological, and utopian type, for example (with the proviso that each of them be understood within its specific historical, cultural context, and not *sub specie aeternitatis*). The specificity of each consists of the simultaneous presence of a certain number of fundamental characteristics or components, a same component obviously being able to belong to several forms of thought. Each brings its own approaches and procedures into play, its various manners of arranging its components, of connecting them. In doing so, it constitutes for itself a corpus of references, a culture.

Certain components can be common to several forms of thought; for example, both to "mysticism" and to "esotericism." With the latter, the "scientific" maintains complex and ambiguous relationships of which certain Nature philosophies are the stake. It is especially interesting to observe the oppositions, the rejections; they not only are due to incompatible components between two forms of thought, but also can result from an epistemological break within one of them. Thus, before theology discarded (section II) its symbolic richness still present in the Middle Ages, for example in the School of Chartres, in that of Oxford, or in the case of a Saint Bonaventure (chapter 1, section II), it was still close to what we here call modern Western esotericism.

The first five of the six characteristics or components enumerated above are not, let it be noted, of a doctrinal order. They appear much rather as receptacles where various forms of the *imaginaire* can find a place. For example, in the matter of "correspondences" we are dealing as much with hierarchies of a Neoplatonic type (the above is placed hierarchically higher than the below) as with more "democratic" views (God is found as much in a seed as anywhere else; heliocentrism changes nothing essential, etc.); in the matter of "transmutation," as much with that of Nature as with that of only humanity; in the matter of cosmogony, with schemes as much emanationist (God creates the universe by emanation of Himself) as creationist (the universe was created *ex nihilo*); in the matter of reincarnation, as much with a defense as with a rejection of this idea; in the matter of attitude to modernity, some easily integrate it, others reject all its values, and so forth. In fact, for most of the representatives of this form of thought, it is less a question of believing than of knowing (*gnosis*) and of "seeing" (by the exercise of active, creative imagination—third component). Thus, to approach the studied field as a series of receptacles for the *imaginaire* appears to us more in accordance with its very nature than to attempt to define it starting from what would be a matter of particular explicit beliefs, professions of faith, doctrines—an attempt that, according to us, could only lead to a dead end. This procedure has, moreover, the advantage of favoring the methodological approaches of the pluri- and transdisciplinary type that permit situating our field within the context of the humanities in general and the history of religions in particular.

V. State of Research and Institutionalization

On this methodological plane, precisely, a number of "generalists" (section III), whose major contributions are quoted in the bibliography appended to this book, have greatly contributed to establish the specialty on solid bases. In the first place, Wouter J. Hanegraaff, as much by his major work, *New Age Religion and Western Culture: Esotericism in the Mirror of Secular Thought* (1996), as by an impressive series of articles subsequently published, all of fundamental importance. He currently stands out as the main scholar among the "generalists" of our specialty—besides the fact that he has also authored various cogent studies on specific authors and currents. Comparable in his approach is Marco Pasi; his scholarly works have hitherto focused principally on the so-called "occultist" current, but he has completed them with very pertinent working models to treat notions such as "occultism" and "magic" in the context of modern Western esotericism (cf. especially his thesis, *La notion de magie dans le courant occultiste en Angleterre [1875–1947]*, 2004). Let us also cite Jean-Pierre Brach for his survey examinations of the historical characteristics proper to esoteric currents, as they manifest themselves in the European cultural arena from the end of the fifteenth century; Andreas Kilcher, who, in studying the various usages of the polysemous term "Kabbalah" in the modern West, has shed new light on the migrations and derivations of modern esoteric currents (*Die Sprachtheorie der Kabbala als ästhetisches Paradigma*, 1998); Olav Hammer, one of whose works has the title, evocative for our purpose: *Claiming Knowledge: Strategies of Epistemology from Theosophy to the New Age* (2001). Noteworthy too is Nicholas Goodrick-Clarke's excellent introduction to our field (*The Western Esoteric Traditions. A Historical Introduction*; 2008).

Still other "generalists" are situated within this body of theoretical thoughts that all rest on a solid work of texts. Among them are Arthur Versluis, by his articles published in his review *Esoterica* and by a number of his works; and Monika Neugebauer-Wölk, who attempts, in particular, to elucidate conceptually and historically the nature of the relationships between esotericism and Christianity. The recent works of Kocku von Stuckrad, notably his book *Was ist Esoterik?* (2005), introduce a model of orientation that is just as "historian," rather different nevertheless from the preceding ones; its application can, in our view, appear problematic as to the specificity of our field— but it is no less stimulating.

This list of "generalists" concerned with methodology is not exhaustive, but rather suggests that the specialty, understood as much *lato sensu* as *stricto sensu* (twenty centuries, or only five), could already have been a subject of academic institutionalization. The process began in 1964. We owe to the Religious Sciences section of the École Pratique des Hautes Études (Paris, Sorbonne) the merit of having, that year, been the first university institution to create within itself a position entitled *Directeur d'Études* [Professor] (that of François Secret) of the History of Christian Esotericism. The name changed in 1979 (with Antoine Faivre) to the History of Esoteric and Mystical Currents in Modern and Contemporary Europe (when Jean-Pierre Brach took over, in 2002, the term *mystical* was deleted from that chair title). At the University of Amsterdam, a Center for History of Hermetic Philosophy and Related Currents (actually, for the History of Western Esotericism as we understand it here) was created in 1999. It has a specific chair (held by Wouter J. Hanegraaff), flanked by two Assistant Professorships [Br: Senior lecturers], a secretary and two PhD lecturers; it thus offers its students a complete academic trajectory. At the University of Lampeter (United Kingdom), a Centre for Western Esotericism saw the light of day in 2002; and in 2006, at that of Exeter (United Kingdom), a chair entitled Western Esotericism, occupied by Nicholas Goodrick-Clarke, forms the basis of the "Exeter Center for the Study of Esotericism" (EXECESO). It too, like the Center in Amsterdam, offers its students a complete academic trajectory. The close collaboration established between Exeter, Amsterdam, and Paris, and of these three with other institutions, is part of a development with considerable impact on scholarship internationally.

Besides these creations properly speaking, several initiatives were taken. For example, at the University of Lausanne (Département inter-facultaire d'Histoire et Sciences des Religions), a biannual program was established in 2003 (by Silvia Mancini), dedicated to an introduction to the field of this specialty. In Germany, at the University Martin Luther of Halle-Wittenberg, research programs were created (notably by Monika Neugebauer-Wölk), dedicated to the esoteric currents of the period of the Enlightenment as well as to the "hermetico-esoteric movements" of the beginning of Modern Times. At Ludwig-Maximilian University of Munich, Hereward Tilton led from 2004 to 2006 a seminar called "Introduction to the History of Western Esotericism." We could give many more examples.

To these initiatives, we may add various symposia, colloquia, and associations.

In the United States, the American Academy of Religion—the largest association of religious sciences in the world—a program unit "Modern Western Esotericism" was instituted for the annual congress of 1980. Several others followed it, among which was "Esotericism" in 1986. It ceased to function in 1993 because of the perennialist orientation of its organizers, strongly criticized by several of the participants. It then made way, starting in 1994, for programs of a historico-critical type directed by James Santucci; first, under the title "Theosophy and Theosophic Thought," then in 1999 under that of "Western Esotericism since the Early Modern Period." Since 2004 this program unit has become "Western Esotericism"; under the direction of Allison Coudert, Wouter J. Hanegraaff, and Cathy Guttierez. It also follows a strictly historian orientation. Let us note that these last reformulations (from 1994 to 2004) coincided with the revival of the process of institutionalization and professionalization in several countries (cf. *supra*), begun in the wake of the creation of the Parisian chair in 1964. Still in the United States, new associations of an international character saw the light of day, which work in this same spirit. Thus, the Association for the Study of Esotericism created in 2002, directed by Arthur Versluis and Allison Coudert; among the conferences that it has organized appears notably Esotericism, Art and Imagination (University of Davis, California, 2006).

Besides these properly American initiatives, in the context of the International Association for the History of Religion (which holds its congress every five years), a workshop Western Esotericism and the Science of Religion (Proceedings published, cf. bibliography) was created in 1995 in Mexico City. Two other workshops followed it: Western Esotericism and Jewish Mysticism (Durban, 2000) and Western Esotericism and Polemics (Tokyo, 2005). The Association for International Research on Esotericism and of the Religious Sciences section of the École Pratique des Hautes Études held the conference Autour de l'oeuvre de Frances A. Yates (1899–1981): Du réveil de la tradition hermétique à la naissance de la science moderne (Paris, 2001). At Esalen (California), a program of four symposia was established: The Varieties of Esoteric Experience (2004), Hidden Intercourse: Eros and Sexuality in Western Esotericism (Proceedings published in 2008), Hidden Truths, Novel Truths (2006), Western Esotericism and Altered States of Consciousness (2007). In such a context are situated one of the nine sessions of the international conference Religious History of Europe and Asia of September 2006 at Bucharest, whose theme was "Hermetic and Esoteric Currents," and the international conference Forms and Currents of Western Esotericism of October 2007 at Venice (Proceedings published in 2008).

Let us mention finally the European Society for the Study of Western Esotericism (http://www.esswe.org/), created in 2002. This place of exchange and information brings together many researchers from the whole world and has already organized two international conferences: Constructing Tradition, Means and Myths of Transmission in Western Esotericism (University of Tübingen, 2007, Proceedings forthcoming), and Capitals of European Esotericism and Transcultural Dialogue (University of Strasbourg, 2009, Proceedings forthcoming).

The list would be long of all the collective works, articles of a methodological and philological nature, and so on, which are of interest to the generalist and which have seen the light of day in various countries for about fifteen years. To some of the publications already mentioned, it is appropriate especially to mention the *Dictionary of Gnosis and Western Esotericism*, published in 2005. Its two volumes comprise some four hundred articles written by about one hundred and eighty collaborators and cover the field of Western esotericism from Late Antiquity until today; cf. *in cauda* the bibliography, which also includes a list of specialized libraries and journals (not least the biannual *Aries. Journal for the Study of Western Esotericism*, published since 2002). And because the bibliography does not include the titles of articles but only of books, it seems appropriate to mention here the copious annual rubric entitled "Bulletin d'histoire des ésotérismes," held by the "generalist" Jerôme Rousse-Lacordaire since 1996 in the *Revue des Sciences philologiques et théologiques* (his book reviews gathered in this "Bulletin" already constitute a wealth of information).

VI. Past and Present Obstacles to the Recognition of This Specific Field

Hence, after a long period of marginalization, this specific field is increasingly the subject of official recognition. However, four obstacles have delayed this recognition, more or less continuing to slow its development.

The first obstacle is the existence of approaches of a religionist/universalist character. This has been sufficiently discussed in section III for it to be superfluous to insist on the necessity, for historians, to distinguish themselves clearly from such approaches—which, obviously, does not imply for as much that they should refrain from making a statement about their philosophical pertinence.

The second obstacle is the "confusionism" favored by the first of the meanings discussed in section I. We often see even serious people, specialists of particular disciplines, employ "esotericism" as a portmanteau (or "blanket") word for lack of anything better, with the complicity of their readers and publishers, to refer to some of the areas they treat (such as *imaginaire*, initiatic or fantasy literature, religious symbolism, artistic works associated with some aura of mystery, etc.) This tendency is due to the more or less implicit adoption of a "received idea" that spread little by little in the West, especially since the nineteenth century. It consists in positing the existence of a sort of counter-culture, vaguely understood as the whole of what is covered by the first of the six meanings of "esotericism." And by the effect of a curious reversal, it happens that this word no longer refers to that whole, but is found summoned to refer strangely to a single aspect of "magic" and/or "occult sciences." For example, in the *Dictionnaire historique de la magie et des sciences occultes* (2006), directed by Jean-Michel Sallmann, appears the entry "Western esotericism." Thus, for Sallmann, "Western esotericism" is one of the aspects of what he understands by "magic" and "occult sciences," on the same level as "Miracles," "Cult of saints," "Unicorn," "Fairies," and so on—entries, among so many others of the same type, presented in this dictionary. In addition, just as we fail to understand why an image, a theme or a motif would be "esoteric" (cf. *supra*, section I, the remarks concerning the first meaning), so it appears to us at least strange to posit that miracles, the cult of saints, the unicorn, fairies (so many images, themes or motifs) come under "magic" and "occult knowledge."

The third obstacle is due to the residual influence of theological models or presuppositions in the study of religions in general and that of Christianity in particular. Even though the History of Religions had begun, since the nineteenth century, to emancipate itself from Christian theology, people had nonetheless long continued to adopt insufficiently critical (mainly crypto-Catholic) views. They saw the esoteric currents as no more than marginal heresies or more or less "condemnable" superstitions—although in fact they generally appear to be much less "marginal" than "transversal." To start from doctrinal elements only perpetuates misunderstandings; with the aid of bits and pieces of theology or metaphysics taken here and there, one can construct a heresy that does not exist and then have a good time criticizing it. Now, even granted that the discourses we here qualify as esoteric sometimes contain heretical propositions with regard to religious institutions, this is in no way what defines these discourses as "esoteric." Indeed, a heresy, in order to be considered as such, must be formulated in terms of concepts incompatible with other concepts that constitute a dogma. Now, esoteric discourses are generally much less of the order of the concept than of the image, and more generally of mythical thought.

Moreover, this form of thought—as springs out from the following chapters—frequently penetrates most of the established religions. Catholicism obviously does not escape it. Contrary to what many works on ecclesiological history would suggest (often only addressing oppositions of the Churches/sect or orthodoxy/heresy type), during the first three centuries of the so-called modern period and until the early eighteenth century, these currents were still part, as in previous centuries, of the general history of Christendom. They constitute, let us recall (*supra*, section II), a dimension—unfortunately too long neglected by historical research—of the Christian culture "visited" by Islam or Judaism. They did not then appear as a counter-culture or a "counter-tradition" that would, by its very nature, have opposed the religious powers in place (it is obviously necessary, however, to study the complex relationships that they maintained with established institutions); nor was this the case for a number of them in the course of the last three centuries. Hence, for the eighteenth century, a "pivotal" period, we cannot talk about an "esoteric front" opposing the defenders of "reason," because, there again, examination of the facts comes to contradict overly simplistic schemes.

Let us add that this idea of "counter-culture" sometimes takes on a distinctly negative connotation, due to the appropriation, by movements of the far right, of certain themes present in the literature of esoteric currents. Now, if Nazi or near-Nazi theoreticians, for example, have made use of such themes, it was in a very limited manner and in distorting them; but this was sufficient to produce an amalgamation in many minds (cf. for example, the fine analysis by Nicholas Goodrick-Clarke, *The Occult Roots of Nazism*, 1985). And if, on the other hand, it is true that thinkers of the extreme right, such as Julius Evola, can feel affinities with perennialism (chapter 5, section II), this does not necessarily mean (as the example of René Guénon is enough to show) that, by its nature, this current would belong with similar forms of extremism. Finally, it bears repeating once again that in the nineteenth century, for example, many representatives of the esoteric currents were politically oriented in a very different direction, indeed, towards forms of socialism.

The fourth obstacle, finally, is connected with the very history of the academic specialties of which the discipline History of Religions is composed. In fact, if this discipline had long since already accepted specialties such as the Gnosticism of Late Antiquity, Jewish theosophies (Jewish Kabbalah, notably), and Muslim theosophies, or again Christian mysticism, it is necessary to say in return that the Western esoteric currents, in particular those of the modern period, have been greatly delayed in entering it fully. Two reasons have contributed this delay: on the one hand, many scholars preferred to concentrate on non-Western religions, thus abandoning the history of Christianity, even understood in a broad sense, to the historiography of the Churches; on the other hand, many tended to identify this field with "mysticism" in general (a portmanteau word, as noted above). In addition, the existence of the aforementioned currents of the modern era found itself, under the influence of theological discourse, eclipsed by the debate initiated under rationalist thought and religion. Then, when new types of rationality emerged, these currents found themselves despite everything relegated to the back shelves of historiography, because they came to disturb or complicate the idea that the history of scientific ideas is reducible to that of a science progressively emancipating itself from the religious. Hence, the esoteric currents long failed to be approached from the angle of their specificity.

Similarly, we note that over the last three decades scholars—mostly sociologists—working on the "New Age" and the New Religious Movements (of which many are, unfortunately, qualified as "sects" by the media and the public authorities) are occasionally prone to call their vast domain "esotericism." This gives rise to the idea that no grounds exist to consider Western esotericism as a specific field of research, because it never does more than relate to objects with which these scholars are already preoccupied. In reality, it intersects theirs only to the extent that the discourses of the "New Age" and the New Religious Movements sometimes come to draw their inspiration from those of the Western esoteric currents of the past.

VII. Perspectives: Throwing New Light on Old Questions

From the account of these factors of delay, in particular the last two, it emerges that the study of this field of research is of a nature to throw new light on old questions, notably by revealing certain "missing links" that the traditional boundaries established between various other specialties could have eclipsed. It incites us to revisit, according to new perspectives, important aspects of the history of religions in the West, in the manner, for example, that Gershom Scholem, in his works on Jewish Kabbalah, could illuminate our perception of Jewish thought with a new day. A comment of Paul Oskar Kristeller seems pertinent here, who wrote, in 1976:

> thanks to the work of Thorndike, of Miss Yates and others, we are no longer terrified when we encounter strange scientific ideas or astrological, alchemical or magical conceptions among the thinkers of past centuries. If we discover ideas of this type in the work of Ficino, we do not reproach him for it, but we simply place him in a vast intellectual tradition that had been too long neglected and avoided by the historians, and which is represented by an extensive and difficult literature, which still needs . . . a great effort of study and exploration. ("L'état présent des études sur Marsile Ficin," in *Platon et Aristote à la Renaissance*, Paris, J. Vrin, 1976)

Indeed, the History of Religions can now take advantage of these updates even better as the general decline in the belief in the "grand narratives" of modernity goes hand in hand with interest in ways of thought that a normative conception of historiography had long discounted. Moreover, a "History of the Western Esoteric Currents" is of a nature to question a certain number of prejudices that are still very current; here are two examples.

The first is that of the relationships maintained, in the West, between religious phenomena and the processes of modernization/secularization. The incompatibility between the former and the latter, which modernist discourse stipulated, already appears contradicted, all concurring to show that the modern esoteric currents (Christian or not), in particular, have proved to have an astonishing capacity of survival by adapting and assimilating themselves. Bound as they were to this general process of religious secularization, they represent a dimension—still often poorly understood—of this society become pluralist. Their study, attentive to a constant interaction of various discourses and to historical discontinuities, thus indeed seems to be of a nature to lie within the project of a revision of the history of the relationships between "religion" and "secularization," which appear much more complex than current modernist views suggested still recently.

The second example is the interest presented by the historicization of the discourses of an "anti-esoterical" character. Indeed, a serious study of these currents properly speaking necessarily implies, by the same token, that of the discourses "for" and "against" them, for or against their representatives, as much in the Christian context as in the secular one (cf. e.g., the collective work *Polemical Encounters*, 2008, *infra*, bibliography). This aspect of historiographical research can only contribute to clarify the emergence and the transformations of concepts like "magic," "occult," and the like, which, for better and for worse, were founding elements as much for the History of Religions as for Anthropology, to the point of becoming an integral part of our ways of thought. It is advisable never to forget, indeed, that Westerners applied similar concepts, still often charged with negative implications, to non-European cultures only after applying them to themselves in a spirit directed, in fact, against their own "inner demons."

Our task is always to re-interrogate these concepts by historicizing them; to question some of the "great paradigms" that often continue to rule our understanding of history; and to make some of the ideological mechanisms still at work in the theoretical heritage of the History of religions subject to an ever-renewed problematicization. The latter has the responsibility to address, notably, the rhetoric of exclusions and the "great taboos" by which the object that we are studying, and others situated in its vicinity, could find themselves relegated to the status of "Other," of the "religiously other."

I

Ancient and Medieval Sources of the Modern Western Esoteric Currents

I. The First Eleven Centuries

1. Alexandrian Hermetism

S cattered works, partly lost, written in Greek in the region of Alexandria, constitute a heterogeneous mass known as the *Hermetica*. Composed over several centuries at the dawn of our era, these treatises deal with astrology, alchemy, the philosophy of Nature, cosmology, and theurgy. A collection dating from the second and third centuries stands out within this body of works, the *Corpus Hermeticum* (CH). It brings together seventeen short treatises. Also part of that body are the *Asclepius* and the "Fragments" attributed to Stobaeus. Their author or legendary inspirer is Hermes Trismegistus, the "thrice great," whom many mythical and contradictory genealogies associate with the name Thoth and the Greek Hermes. He would have lived in the time of Moses, and the Egyptians would have been indebted to him for their laws and their knowledge. The Middle Ages did not know the CH, rediscovered at the Renaissance, but only the *Asclepius* (in its Latin translation).

Despite the speculative aspect of the CH, we should not seek a unified doctrine in it. As we move from one treatise to the next, we find contradictions and discrepancies, because they are the work of different authors. The most famous treatise is the *Poimandres*, or *Pimander*, always published as the first in the series of those comprising the *CH*. It develops a cosmogony and an anthropology on a mode of illumination and revelation. Among the prominent themes are those of the fall and the reintegration, and of memory in its relationships with a form of "magical" imagination.

The *CH* itself does not treat alchemy strictly speaking. It seems that, unknown to Pharaonic Egypt, it developed as an extension of Hermeticist astrology, in particular starting from the notion of sympathy linking each planet to its corresponding metal (until about the second century B.C., alchemy remained a technique associated with the practice of goldsmithing). With Bolos of Mendes, in the second century B.C., it took a philosophical turn and sometimes presented itself in a light of revelation—as a "revealed" science. Zozimus of Panapolis (third or early fourth century), of whom twenty-eight treatises have been preserved, developed a visionary alchemy, followed in this by Synesius (fourth century), Olympiodorus (sixth century), and Stephanos of Alexandria (seventh century) in whom alchemy is also considered a spiritual exercise.

2. Other Non-Christian Currents

To Alexandrian Hermetism, four other non-Christian currents are added, important in the genesis of modern esotericism. These currents are, to begin with, the neo-Pythagoreanism of the two first centuries of our era; it would never cease to reappear subsequently under different forms of arithmosophy. Then we have Stoicism, which extended over nearly two centuries, one aspect of which bears on the universe understood as an organic totality guaranteeing harmony between terrestrial and celestial matters. Third, we have Neoplatonism that, from Plotinus (205–270) to the fifth century, taught methods that permit gaining access to a supersensible reality, constructing or describing this reality in its structure. Porphyry (273–305), Iamblichus (*On the Egyptian Mysteries*, toward 300), and Proclus (412–486) appear among the most visible Neoplatonists in later esoteric literature. In the fifth or the sixth century, a cosmological text of a few pages was drawn up, *Sepher Yetzirah* (*Book of Creation*), a prefiguration of what would be the medieval Kabbalah proper (it contains notably the first-known introduction of the famous so-called Tree of the Sephiroth).

Added to this was an intense intellectual activity in the Arab world, connected with the rapid expansion of Islam. The Arabic *Epistles* of the "Sincere Brethern" (ninth century) contain many speculations of a cosmological nature. Starting in this same century, Neoplatonic texts and the *Hermetica* were translated into Arabic. They gave rise to the appearance of original works (*Theology of Aristotle*, ninth century; *Picatrix* [tenth century], an encyclopedia of magical knowledge partly of Greek origin; *Turba Philosophorum* [*Assembly of the Philosophers*], a compilation of discourses on alchemy; "Book of the Secrets of Creation," ca. 825, which contains the first version of the famous text of the *Emerald Tablet*).

3. In Christian Thought of the First Eleven Centuries

Was there a "Christian esotericism" understood as a more or less secret set of teachings delivered by Jesus to his disciples, and was this teaching of an essentially Jewish type: These are questions still debated. In his *Stromateis* ("Miscellanies"), Clement of Alexandria (160–215), whose Hellenistic Christianity is tinged with Jewish mysticism, emphasized the importance of *gnosis* understood as "knowledge" that supports and transcends faith. Origen (185–254) advocated a constant effort of interpretation, on several levels, of the texts of the Holy Scriptures in order to pass from faith to this *gnosis*.

Marginal to the more or less official Christianity that both represent, Gnosticism is a vast current that takes different forms. Their common theme is deliverance from evil through the destruction of our universe and the elevation of our soul toward the celestial spheres. Unlike Basilides and Valentinus, other Gnostics of the second century, like Marcion, taught a dualist conception (Evil is ontologically equal to Good) of humankind and the world. We find it again in another form in the so-called Manichaean current issued from Mani (second century). A metaphysical pessimism marks the thinking—very rich, all permeated with a luxuriant *imaginaire*—of Gnosticism, which was a source of Bulgarian Bogomilism in the tenth century and hence of Catharism. In the following period, three names stand out. First is Pseudo-Dionysius (Dionysius Aeropagita), whose three main works (*Mystical Theology*, *Divine Names*, and *Celestial Hierarchy*), written in Greek in the sixth century and partly inspired by the ideas of Proclus, are devoted to angelology and would remain a standard reference on the subject. Second is Maximus the Confessor who, one century later, explained the works of Pseudo-Dionysius. And third, in the ninth century, is the Irish monk Johannes Scottus Eriugena, author of the *Periphyseon* (*On the Division of Nature*). The latter is one of the most important intellectual constructions of the Middle Ages, which would ensure the transmission of a sort of "dynamized" Platonism in many ways close to the Jewish Kabbalah soon to flourish in Spain (section III, 1).

II. In Medieval Thought

1. Aspects of Theology

The twelfth century discovered Nature in a light of analogy. Only recently accessible to the West, Arabian knowledge favored this orientation. In the School of Chartres, especially in Bernardus Silvestris (*De mundi universitate*, 1147) and William of Conches (toward 1080–1145), there was still no hiatus between metaphysical principles and cosmology. The period saw the birth of the masterpiece of Alain de Lille (1128–1203), *De planctu naturae*; the dazzling and we could say proto-theosophical illustrated texts of Hildegard of Bingen (1098–1179), particularly her *Scivias*. Appearing also were the *Clavis Physicae* and the *Elucidarium* of Honorius Augustodunensis (Honoré d'Autun), besides many other similar creations.

If, in this Romanesque period, correspondences, symbolic imagination, Nature and ways of spiritual transformation occupy an important place, the Franciscan spirit that emerged in the thirteenth century came, by its love of Nature, to reinforce this tendency. The School of Oxford contributed much to it (the theology of light in Robert Grosseteste, alchemy and astrology in Roger Bacon [see section II, 3], etc.), as well as the work of the Italian Saint Bonaventure (1217–1274) whose theological work develops a theory of the "coincidence of opposites" prefiguring that of Nicholas of Cusa (section II, 2).

When, toward 1300, the penetration of Arabic texts into Latinity was practically completed, we witness the triumph of Latin Averroism in Christian theology—that is to say, of the thought of the Arab Averroes (1126–1198), interpreter of Aristotle—to the detriment of the influence of the Persian Avicenna (980–1037). Whence, a form of rationality appeared in theology, which would deeply mark Western minds. Thus, the Christian and Islamic twelfth century increasingly "theologized" the Aristotelian "secondary causes" (especially cosmology) in a metaphysical direction, which would render problematic the relationship between metaphysical principles and Nature. This problematization would favor, in the Renaissance, the emergence of the esoteric currents proper (cf. Introduction, section II).

2. "Sums" and Universal Syntheses

Many *summae* are compendia of marvels and observations about the "powers" operant in the mineral, plant, and animal kingdoms. They adumbrate the *philosophia occulta* of the Renaissance (this is the case, e.g., of the *Speculum naturale* of Vincent of Beauvais, 1245, or the *De proprietatibus rerum* of Bartholomaeus Anglicus, ca. 1230). However, there also are "sums" appearing as systems of thought, as grand philosophical syntheses. Not all of them are part of this tendency, as for example, that of Thomas Aquinas.

The work of the Calabrian abbot Joachim da Fiore (ca. 1135–1202), who distinguishes three great periods of Universal History (the reign of the Father, that of the Son, and that—yet to come—of the Holy Spirit), would enjoy a considerable vogue in modern times, in particular by the use that philosophers of History would make of it. Let us cite further the *Ars Magna* of Raymundus Lullus (Ramon Llull, toward 1232/3–1310; section II, 3): a combinatory "art" with universal pretentions, marked by medieval Neoplatonism such as Johannes Scottus Eriugena had transmitted it (section I,3). At the end of the Middle Ages, Nicholas of Cusa heralded the Hermetism of the Renaissance through his idea of a fundamental unity of the religions (*De pace fidei*, 1453) and put forth a world system, a theory of "opposites" in which the infinitely great coincides with the infinitely small—a "total" science, encompassing astrology as well.

3. Hermetism, Astrology, and Alchemy

Many were the works of magic, like the *Picatrix* (of Arabian origin, as we have seen [section II, 2], which became the object of Latin translations and of adaptations) or those belonging to *Ars notoria*, the art of invoking angels. The *CH* was lost until the Renaissance, but the *Asclepius* was available in a Latin version and other texts circulated in Alexandrian Hermetist milieux. One of the most widely known, the *Liber XXIV philosophorum*, dates from the twelfth century, while the names Roger of Hereford and John of Sevilla were prominent in astrology. However, this system of knowledge was not essential in a world still imbued with the divine: Dante placed two of the great astrologers of the thirteenth century in his hell: Michael Scot and Guido Bonatti. At the beginning of the fourteenth, Ramon Llull (section II, 2) made an important place for astrology in his *Ars Magna*, as did Peter of Abano in his *Conciliator* (1303). Cecco d'Ascoli (1269–1327), another famous astrologer, was burnt at the stake in Florence. Pierre d'Ailly (1350–1420) wanted to elevate astrology to the level of a "natural theology" supposed to illustrate its complex relationships with Christian knowledge and thought.

As for alchemy, it practically did not reappear in Europe before the twelfth century; Islam reintroduced it there through the intermediary of Spain. The end of the thirteenth saw two alchemical texts circulating in Latin, from which much inspiration would subsequently be drawn: the *Turba Philosophorum*, of Arabian origin, which has ancient alchemists in dialogue; the *Summa*, a body of writings attributed to the Arabian Geber; and the speculations of Roger Bacon (*Opus tertium*, 1267). The *Aurora consurgens* is attributed by legend to Thomas Aquinas. Let us cite further the works attributed to the Catalan Arnau de Vilanova (ca. 1235–1311), in particular his *Rosarium Philosophorum*.

Alchemical literature then began to proliferate rapidly, remaining abundant until at least the seventeenth century. It was notably represented by many treatises attributed to Ramon Llull starting in the fourteenth century, and which are not by him; by John Dastin, Petrus Bonus (*Pretiosa inargarita novella*, ca. 1330), and Nicolas Flamel (1330–1417). With Flamel are associated legends that continue to cause much ink to flow. George Ripley then followed (*The Compound of Alchemy*, 1470; *Medulla alchimiae*, 1476) and Bernardus Trevisanus (1406–1490). As in the late Hellenistic period, certain forms of alchemy, in the Middle Ages, already give the impression of unfolding on two planes: operative and spiritual.

III. Initiatic Quests and Arts

1. Jewish Kabbalah

The influence of the Kabbalah in the Latin world would be considerable from the Renaissance onwards (chapter II, section I, 2). Succeeding the *Sepher Yetsirah* (section I, 2), a compilation of Kabbalistic materials made in Provence in the twelfth century comes to constitute the first exposition of the Kabbalah properly speaking, the *Bahir*, which orientates the latter in the double direction of a *gnosis* of Eastern origin and of a form of Neoplatonism. Numbers and letters of the Old Testament are there the object of a hermeneutics capable of procuring knowledge of the relationships between the world and God, according to an interpretative method that suggests seeing in each word and letter of the Torah a meaning with multiple ramifications. Kabbalistic literature was then enriched with what would remain its fundamental book, the *Sepher ha-Zohar* ("Book of Splendor"), appearing in Spain shortly after 1275. Compilation probably due to Moses of Leon, it represents the summit of Jewish Kabbalah, that is to say, of a speculative mysticism applied to the knowledge and to the description of the mysterious works of God. The *Zohar* considerably extended the Talmudic dimension relative to the tasks or rites for developing a divino-cosmic mythology from which Renaissance thought would profit. Finally, the great mystic Abraham Abulafia (1240–1291), born in Saragossa, taught a meditation technique of an initiatic and symbolic nature that also included physical exercises.

2. Chivalry and Initiatic Societies

The art of the church builders was transmitted in lodges to which modern Freemasonry would often claim to be the heir. Obligations, or "duties," of the masons constitute the Old Charges, of which the texts that have come down to us (the *Regius*, toward 1390, and the *Cooke*, toward 1410) discuss geometry as a script of God that arose simultaneously with the origins of the world.

Also initiatic is chivalry in some of its aspects—to which Templar sites, such as Tomar, in Portugal, seem to bear testimony. However, we must take care not to confuse history and fiction; the destruction of the Order of the Temple in 1312 gave rise to a Templar myth that does not correspond to the facts, just as the Crusade led against the Albigensians in 1207 gave rise to all sorts of legends concerning their alleged "esotericism." In reality, the latter is found much less in these Orders or these movements properly speaking than in the inspired discourses of which they were subsequently the subject, especially starting in the Enlightenment. Thus, the symbols of the Order of the Golden Fleece founded in 1429 by Philip the Good would serve to revive the myth of Jason in the Western *imaginaire*, notably in alchemical literature and, from the second half of the eighteenth century onward, in certain Higher Grades of Freemasonry (chapter III, section III, 1, 2). Let us cite finally the Brethren of the Free Spirit (of Amalric of Bene, also called Amalric of Chartres), starting about 1206; and especially the Friends of God gathered around the layperson Rulman Merswin (1307–1382) in their Alsatian cloister called the Green Island.

3. The Arts

In the twelfth and the thirteenth centuries, churches and cathedrals deploy a visionary theology full of theophanies and metamorphoses. Their symbolism rests on a subtle knowledge of the relationships uniting God, humankind, and the universe. However, let us not attribute to their architects and builders more intentions than they had, despite a few possible references to alchemy (thus, on the bas-reliefs of the central portal of Notre Dame de Paris) or to astrology (tower of the

Sun and the Moon in the cathedral of Chartres, signs of the zodiac in that of Antwerp, etc.).

Alchemy reappeared in the fourteenth century in the form of beautiful illuminated manuscripts, such as that of Constantinus and at the beginning of the fifteenth the *Aurora consurgens*, the "Book of the Holy Trinity," and so on. In architecture, some twentieth-century observers wish to see a true "philosophical dwelling" ("*demeure philosophale*"; chapter V, section I, 1) in the palace of Jacques Coeur at Bourges (first half of the fifteenth century). Astrology was present in art in the very widespread form of plates representing the "children of the planets"; and playing cards, which appeared toward 1375, began from the early fifteenth century to serve as symbolic systems in relationship to gods and planets.

Initiation, secrecy, love, and illuminated knowledge blended in a chivalrous *imaginaire* of which the first great literary expression developed around the legendary King Arthur; this is the *Matter of Britain*, whose heroes are Arthur, Perceval, Lancelot, and the Fisher King. Initiatic and symbolic scenarios are even more characteristic of Grail literature properly speaking. Emerging somewhere around 1180 with the book of Chrétien de Troyes and Robert de Boron, it associates Western traditions of a chivalrous type with Celtic and Druidic elements (thus, the *Vita Merlini* in the twelfth century), and a form of Christianity, notably the virtues of Christ's blood collected by Joseph of Arimathea. Then, between 1200 and 1210, Wolfram von Eschenbach devoted to the Grail and to Chivalry his *Parzival*, in which certain elements of alchemy and Hermetism are identifiable.

If not always alchemical, at least initiatic, is the Grail quest told in *Der Junge Titurel* by Albrecht von Scharfenberg, a long epic written soon after 1260. It contains a striking evocation of the image of the Temple of Solomon and the Heavenly Jerusalem (let us note here that the Grail theme would be practically absent from the thematic range of modern Western esoteric currents until the late nineteenth century). Finally, alchemical connotations are not lacking in the *Roman de la Rose*, begun by Guillaume de Lorris, continued by Jean de Meung and whose writing extends from 1230 to 1285; we see there displayed a rich symbolic universe, which miniatures and illuminations would come to further embellish.

2

Esotericism in the Heart of the Renaissance and the Flames of the Baroque

I. A Discovery of Humanism: *Philosophia Perennis*

I. Re-emergence and Success of the *Corpus Hermeticum*

Toward 1450, in Florence, Cosimo de Medici entrusted Marsilio Ficino (1433–1499; section I, 3) to create a Platonic Academy, and about a decade later he asked him to translate, even before any of the works of Plato, the *Corpus Hermeticum* (CH, see chapter 1, section I, 1) of which a certain number of treatises had just been discovered in Macedonia. Published in 1471, this Latin translation went through no less than twenty-five editions until 1641, to which those of other translations may be added. Common to many commentators of the period—starting with Ficino himself—was the assumption that these treatises, and their "author" Hermes Trismegistus, belonged to a very remote period, that of Moses. Many considered the treatises an adumbration of Christianity and thought they detected in them the presence of a teaching that would be an expression of a *philosophia perennis*, or "eternal philosophy," in which this Hermes would have been one of the links in a chain of prestigious names.

In the Renaissance, this characteristic represents one of the ways in which several modern esoteric currents would orientate their obsessive quest for origins. Hence, the rediscovery of Alexandrian

Hermetism contributed to give rise to a form of religious universalism previously espoused by Nicholas of Cusa (chapter 1, section II, 2). As a result, Hermetism would subsequently flourish best in periods of tolerance (it was to find itself stifled in England; for example, during the Puritan period, under Edward VI and under Mary Tudor).

Among the main exegetes and editors of the *CH* in the sixteenth century, we find, besides the name of Ficino, those of Lodovico Lazzarelli (1447–1500; *Diffinitiones Asclepii*, 1482, *Crater Hermetis*, composed in 1492–1494; section III, 2); François Foix-Candale (1512–1594; *Pimander*, 1579), Hannibal Rossel (*Pymander*, 1585–1590), Symphorien Champier (1471–1538; *Liber de quadruplici vita*, 1507); Francesco Giorgi (1466–1540; *De Harmonia mundi*, 1525; *infra*, 2, and section III, 1), Heinrich Cornelius Agrippa (1486–1535; *De occulta philosophia*, 1533; *Oratio in praelectionem Trismesgisti*, 1535; section I, 2), Philippe du Plessis-Mornay (1549–1623; *De la vérité de la religion chrétienne*, 1582) and Francesco Patrizi (1529–1597). The purpose of the latter, like that of Giordano Bruno (1548–1600; section III, 1), was to restore true Christianity by incorporating the Hermetic writings and the Zoroastrian oracles with it (*Nova de universis philosophia*, 1591). This neo-Alexandrian Hermetism also tinges the work of John Dee (1527–1609; *Monas Hieroglyphica*, 1554; section III, 1).

In 1614, a famous Genevan philologist, Isaac Casaubon, demonstrated that the texts of the *CH* date from no earlier than the very first centuries of our era (let us mention, however, that other exegetes had noted this a few years before). Thus suspected of being much more recent than formerly believed, they found fewer admirers and commentators. Some Hermetists became aware of this discovery only little by little, while others ignored it deliberately. An English translation by John Everard (1650–1657) of the *CH* was published in 1650 and remained influential (it was based on Ficino's Latin translation). Robert Fludd (1574–1637) made the *CH* one of the foundations of his theosophy (*Utriusque cosmic historia*, 1617–1621; section III, 1), and Ralph Cudworth (*The True Intellectual System of the Universe*, 1678) used it to support his metaphysics. Athanasius Kircher, who studied its relationship with ancient Egyptian traditions (*Oedipus aegyptiacus* 1652–1654), contributed to reinforcing the wave of egyptophilia of modern times. Finally, this Hermetism also found its way into scientific discourses—thus, in Copernicus, who mentions the Trismegistus in his *De Revolutionibus* of 1543, in Johannes Kepler (*Harmonices Mundi*, 1619, section III, 1, 2)—and in the humanist Richard Burton (*Anatomy of Melancholy*, 1621).

2. Christian Kabbalah

The ancient Jewish Kabbalah had placed greater emphasis on theogony and cosmogony than on the history of salvation and messianism. This second aspect took precedence over the first after the diaspora consecutive to the decree of 1492 that expulsed the Jews from Spain and entailed a cultural exodus especially directed toward Italy. Thus, Isaac Luria (1534–1572) orientated the reading of Kabbalah in this new direction that would later gain widespread acceptance in the Jewish tradition. This diaspora greatly contributed to make Jewish Kabbalah known and to stimulate the development of its reading in a Christian sense—a reading that did not begin with the Florentine Giovanni Pico della Mirandola (1463–1494; section I, 3), but it really emerged with him. Pico did not attempt a Christian interpretation of Jewish Kabbalah but instead developed a hermeneutics of Christianity by using methods that the Jews employed to discover hidden truths in the revealed texts. In this, his "theses" (*Conclusiones*, introduced in 1486) mark the beginning of this current; in them he asserted that the Judaism of the Kabbalah is identifiable with Christianity and that "no science proves the divinity of Christ better than Kabbalah and magic."

At this moment (1492–1494), Jacques Lefèvre d'Étaples wrote *De magia naturali*, in which he deals with magic and Kabbalah. Johannes Reuchlin wrote *De Verbo mirifico* (1494, followed by his *De arte cabbalistica* in 1517), and the converted Jew Paulus Ricius submitted his translations of Hebrew texts into Latin (*Porta lucis*, 1515) to those curious about arithmosophy, theosophical exegesis, and divine names. Kabbalah, magic, Hermetism, and alchemy are interwoven to some extent in the daring and celebrated synthesis (in fact, a vast compilation) of Heinrich Cornelius Agrippa (1486–1535; section I, 1), *De Occulta philosophia*, written in 1510 and published in 1533, which would remain one of the great "classics" of modern Western esotericism until today. Celebrated also in its period is the *De arcanis catholicae veritatis* (1518) of the Franciscan Pietro Galatino. Other Franciscans practiced a Christian Kabbalah, such as Jehan Thenaud, who wrote at the request of François I or especially Francesco Giorgio (or Zorzi; section I, 1), who dedicated his *De Harmonia mundi* (1525) to Clement VII. That book was translated into French (1578) under the title *De l'Harmonie du Monde*, by Guy Le Fèvre de La Boderie (section I, 1), and was followed in 1536 by Giorgio's *Problemata*.

The monumental work of Francesco Giorgio must not make us overlook the writings of Cardinal Aegidius of Viterbo, a genius of universal culture (*Libellus*, 1517; *Scechinah*, 1530). The most famous French representative of this current is Guillaume Postel (1510–1581), excluded from the Company of Jesus in 1545. In 1553, he gave an annotated translation of the *Zohar*, followed in 1548 by an *Interprétation du candélabre de Moyse*; many other books, including the first Latin translation of the *Sepher Yetzirah*, are to the credit of this prolific genius. Christian Kabbalah was implanted in England predominantly in the seventeenth century, with James Bonaventure Hepburn (*Virga aurea*, 1616) and Robert Fludd (*Summum Bonum*, 1629; section III, 1). Father Marin Mersenne attempted (*Observationes*, 1632), in refuting Francesco Giorgio, Fludd, and Postel, to combat what had almost become a fashion. Finally, the *Cabala denudata* (1677–1684), of Knorr von Rosenroth, contains a partial translation of the *Zohar* into Latin, abounds in theosophical considerations and texts, picks up the torch of Reuchlin, Postel and their like, and would serve as a standard reference to many subsequent kabbalizing theosophers.

3. *Homo Universalis*: Activity, Dignity, and Synthesis

Thanks to thinkers such as Pico and Ficino, the Renaissance, at its beginnings, discovered original horizons, like Hermetism and Jewish Kabbalah. Ways of stepping back from the cultural and spiritual fields inherited from the Middle Ages, *philosophia perennis* and Christian Kabbalah further expressed the need to practice a "concordance" of various traditions worldwide and favored the tendency to imagine corespondences at play on all levels of reality. This attitude was accompanied by an exaltation of human labor and human activities.

Thus, in the case of Ficino, Hermetism and Platonism served to extol the greatness of humanity and to construct a cosmosophy (*Theologia platonica*, 1469–1474; *De vita coelitus comparanda*, 1489; section I, 1; section III, 1).

Pico, a multitalented polymath, intended to create a harmonious synthesis of Plato, Aristotle, and Christianity, but also to reinterpret the latter through "Kabbalah and magic" (section I, 2). Whereas Kabbalah relates to the "initial causes," magic, which acts on the "second" or "intermediary causes"—for example, on the stars—brings together the natural and the religious, and places the branches of knowledge and of religion on a common trunk. However, despite the visionary cosmology that he presents in his *Heptaplus*, the very eclectic curiosities of Pico have little bearing on either Nature philosophy or mathematics. His spirited critique of deterministic astrology reminds individuals that they are free. Moreover, in his *Oratio de dignitate hominis* (1486), he declares that we are not only a microcosm reflecting a macrocosm, but also beings endowed with the faculty of making decisions about our destiny and about the place we are to occupy within the hierarchy of beings.

II. The Germanic Contribution: Nature Philosophy and Theosophy

I. Paracelsism

In the Germanic countries of the sixteenth century, Lutheranism tended to dampen the reception of Neoplatonism, neo-Alexandrian Hermetism, and Kabbalah. But this was compensated for by a "magical" vision of the world, very widespread in the Europe of those times, and notably by the appearance and the development of a Nature philosophy of which Theophrastus Bombastus von Hohenheim, known as Paracelsus (1493/1494–1541), is the most illustrious representative. This Swiss spent his life traveling through Europe, studying Nature, caring for the sick, and writing. Appointed professor at the Academy of Medicine of Basel in 1527, he did not remain there for long, having caused offense by his proposals of reform. Besides, he did not use

Latin but German, and, to make it worse, he attacked the authority of the Ancients (like that of Galen), which he aimed to replace with "experience"—in the sense of "practical experimentation." In dying, he left a considerable body of work (*Volumen paramirum, Philosophia Sagax*, and many other titles) of which only a small part was published in his lifetime. Not until the publication of the Huser edition (1589) had most of his works got into print.

While in the Neoplatonic tradition we pass from the first divine principle to matter through a series of degrees, Nature, according to Paracelsus, is founded directly on divine omnipotence. Nature is an epiphany. Moreover, Paracelsus is comparable to the Neoplatonists Plotinus and Proclus by his qualitative concept of time, "which flows in a thousand ways," each individual thing possessing its own rhythm. Although not practicing alchemy, he conceived the universe in "chemical" terms; everything, including the stars, has been created "chemically" and hence continues to evolve—furthermore, Western alchemy initiated a turning point under his influence. An instrument of the knowledge of the world, of humanity, of the very Creator, it would increasingly become a totalizing vision. By the same token, this "science of Hermes" found itself connected as though organically to astrology, which Paracelsus did not conceive as a system of influences or physical determinations, but rather as a blueprint of universal interdependences, the stars finding themselves at least as much inside human beings as outside them.

A principle of knowledge, an organ of our soul, called the "Light of Nature," reveals the *magnalia Dei* or the correlations between humanity, the Earth, the stars, the metals, and the chemical elements. Just as our physical body takes nourishment from the elements, so our invisible sidereal body takes nourishment by letting the *Gestirn* (the spirit of the stars) act in it. The task not only of "Doctors" (physicians), but also of people in general, is to learn how to receive this "light of Nature" in themselves. Like Pico and Ficino (section I, 3), Paracelsus understood human existence in a dynamic perspective, as a task to accomplish. Hence, emphasis was placed on individual responsibility, whereas in the Middle Ages human beings instead felt immersed within the flow of a preordained community.

The influence of this thought was considerable. It radiated throughout several branches of knowledge, especially starting at the end of the century. The esoteric currents are not the only ones concerned; what would little by little become chemistry in the modern sense is, too, as is medicine—and this despite strong oppositions (e.g., that of Thomas Erastus, *Disputationes*, 1572–1573). Most of the great continuators of Paracelsus, notably Gérard Dorn (*Congeries Paracelsicae*, 1581; section II, 2; section III, 2), contributed to make him known in the second half of the sixteenth century and inherited from him his idea of the complementarities of the two "Books," namely, the Bible and Nature. Among other very numerous names appearing in his wake are Oswald Croll (*Basilica chymica*, 1609) and Jan Baptista van Helmont (*Ortus mediciniae*, 1648).

2. Jacob Boehme and the Theosophical Current

By the accent put on the "Light of Nature," Paracelsism already heralds the great Christian theosophical current. It is again in Germany that the latter appeared. It is prefigured by such persons as Agrippa, Francesco Giorgio, and Guillaume Postel, whom we have already met; by Lambert Daneau (*Physice christiana*, 1575); by speculative alchemists such as Gérard Dorn (*Clavis totius philosophiae*, 1567; section II, 1; section III, 2); by Heinrich Khunrath whose *Amphithatrum Sapientiae Aeternae* (1595 and 1609) is illustrated by a series of plates become famous; and by Valentin Weigel (*Der Güldene Griff*, 1578; *Dialogus de Christianismo*, 1584), who strove to weave together the Rheno-Flemish mystical tradition and a concrete thought of a Paracelsian type (cf. also *infra*, 3, on Arndt).

Christian theosophy shares the characteristics enumerated above (introduction, section IV) with the other modern Western esoteric currents. It nevertheless possesses certain characteristics that, taken together, serve to specify its originality within this esoteric landscape and that, so it seems to us, come down to three.

1. *The God–Humanity–Nature triangle*: Theosophical speculation pertains simultaneously to God, the nature of God (notably the intra-divine processes), Nature (external, intellectual, or material) and

human beings (their origin, their place in the universe, and in the economy of salvation).

2. *Direct access to higher worlds* and this, by virtue of a "creative imagination" (introduction, section IV) that can lead to a specific experience, *Zentralschau* or "central vision." The *Zentralschau*, a type of altered state of consciousness, is illuminative; it permits embracing in one stroke, as though intuitively, the totality of what constitutes the "triangle" mentioned above; the theosophers that do not have the direct experience themselves always refer to those of their predecessors who were gratified with it.

3. *The primacy of the mythical:* Theosophers practice a permanent and creative hermeneutic of the "texts of origin" (those of the Bible), which serve them as supports for meditation. They achieve this by privileging the mythical elements (that is to say, stories in images) of these texts (e.g., those that we find in *Genesis*, the vision of Ezekiel, and the *Apocalypse*).

The first great representative of the theosophical current properly speaking is Jacob Boehme (1575–1624). A shoemaker of Goerlitz, in Silesia, he had an experience of *Zentralschau* in 1610, triggered by the contemplation of sunlight on a pewter vessel. This determined his spiritual vocation and as an author. *Aurora* (1612), the first book that this illumination had inspired in him, circulated in manuscript and caused him trouble with the Protestant authorities. His following writings had the same effect. Only *Der Weg zu Christo* was printed during his lifetime, in 1624, and the first almost complete edition (by Johann Georg Gichtel, cf. *infra*) of his books came out in 1682. From this prolific work, one of the most impressive in German baroque prose, let us cite (only the titles are in Latin) *De Tribus Principiis* (1619), *De signatura rerum* (1621), *Mysterium Magnum* (1623).

Boehme is not a humanist and, if he is dependent on influences, it is those of Paracelsus, alchemy, and a little bit of Kabbalah. In contrast to a medieval and even Neoplatonic conception of God, he does not conceive of the latter as static but as the place of a passionate struggle of opposing principles. Before Being, there "was" the *Ungrund*—that is to say, the "fathomless" Godhead that ontologically 'precedes' Divinity (God) proper. It is not Reason but a principle, an obscure Will, which finds itself at the foundation of Being. Boehme therefore does not recognize as a supreme entity the *deitas* such as Meister Eckhart conceived it, and which escaped any becoming. Instead, he views it as a fire of a Heraclitean type, a principle that is never in *esse* but always in *fieri*, which "sees" in its living mirror, in the divine Wisdom or Sophia, the potential world. Thus, created by this vision, the divine image then desires, magically engenders, the temporal image.

In the West, sophiology, in other words, the discourses inspired by this character in the Old Testament (see *Book of Wisdom, Proverbs,* etc.), had not yet become the subject of so many speculations, but the *Amphitheatrum* of Khunrath, published in 1595 (cf. *supra*), could have set Boehme on this path. Sophia is almost everywhere present on the great spans of this baroque cathedral that is the work of the Silesian shoemaker. She finds herself associated there with the themes of the fall of Lucifer and of Adam, with the spiritual corporeity of the angels, with the idea that all exterior form is language or *Figur*, and with grandiose evocations of the seven *Quellgeister* or "source-spirits" structuring the relationships between God, humanity, and the universe.

This "prince of Christian theosophy," as he has often been called, enjoyed a certain success in the general turmoil of seventeenth-century Germany. But in other countries, too, theosophy would continue to flourish, irrigated by the thought of Boehme, with Johann Georg Gichtel (1638–1710; *Theosophia practica*, published only in 1722; section III, 3), Gottfried Arnold (*Das Geheimniss der göttlichen Weissheit oder Sophia*, 1700; section III, I, 1), Pierre Poiret (*L'Économie divine ou Système universel*, 1687), Antoinette Bourignon (*Oeuvres* published by Poiret, 1679–1684), John Pordage (*Sophia*, 1675; *Theologia mystica,* 1683), Jane Leade (*A Fountain of Gardens*, 1700)—and many others. Besides theosophy properly speaking, various authors and currents were receptive to Boehme and to Paracelsus, whose teachings seemed to favor a union of faith and knowledge.

3. The First Rosy-Cross

The first Rosicrucian text appeared in 1614, at Cassel (Germany). It was an anonymous manifesto of thirty-eight pages in German, titled *Fama Fraternitatis* "of the praiseworthy order of the Rose Cross," addressed to "all the scholars of Europe" (but this text had already circulated for about four years in manuscript form). We find in it a critique of the spiritual situation of Europe, accompanied by considerations on a possible redemption owing not to the Churches but to a spiritual science in which heart and knowledge would find union. Added to hints of Christian Kabbalah and Pythagoreanism, as well as a strong stamp of Paracelsism, is the biography of a mythical character, C.R.C., a great traveler who would have sojourned in Arabia, in Egypt, and then returned home to Germany to found the said Fraternity there. One hundred and twenty years after his death, in 1604 according to this text, his tomb containing magical formulas and secrets of life would have been found.

In 1615, the *Fama Fraternitatis* was republished in Frankfurt with another text, also anonymous, the *Confessio Fraternitatis*, whose authors observe that the age has entered the sign of Mercury, the "Lord of the Word." They suggest that they are about to reveal part of the Adamic language by means of which people can discover the hidden meanings of the Bible and, at the same time, of creation because the Scriptures are "the Compendium and the quintessence of the whole world." The third text, *Chymische Hochzeit Christiani Rosencreutz Anno 1459* (The Chemical Wedding of Christian Rosenkreutz in the Year 1459), published in 1616 and also anonymous, is an initiatic novel whose hero, Christian Rosenkreutz, undertakes a journey in which the hierogamy of Christ and of His Church, of God with His creation, are described in alchemical metaphors. This fine baroque novel has never ceased to stimulate new works of exegesis.

The first two of these three texts were the work of several authors at this time of great crisis that led to the Thirty Years War. Among them were, in all likelihood, Tobias Hess (1568–1614) and Johann Valentin Andreae (1586–1654). Hess was known as a medical doctor. Andreae (1586–1654), who belonged to an important dynasty of Swabian Lutheranism, is the undisputed author of the novel published in 1616. He left at his death a rather considerable body of work. In his lifetime, he found himself prey to a great deal of harassment because the Protestant authorities strongly suspected him of being the source of the Rosicrucian myth that, with the publication of the two manifestoes (the *Fama* and the *Confessio*), enjoyed overwhelming success.

Indeed, a great many writings either favorable to the contents of these two texts or directed against them immediately appeared in various countries. We count more than two hundred of them between 1614 and 1620, and about nine hundred up to the beginning of the nineteenth century. Among the most important authors having immediately defended and spread the "Rosicrucian" ideas, were Robert Fludd (*Apologia* [Rosae Crucis], 1516; section III, 1), Theophilus Schweighart (*Speculum Sophicum Rhodo Stauroticum*, 1618), and Jan Amos Comenius (*Christianiae societatis imago*, 1620). With Comenius, the irenic project of Andreae, which did not go beyond Germany and the Lutheran confession, "took on planetary dimensions and heralded the humanitarianism of Freemasonry" (R. Edighoffer). In fact, the ideas sown by Comenius took shape in 1660 with the founding of the Royal Society of London (indeed the English, like the Germans, then proved more receptive than did the French to the introduction of Rosicrucian ideas).

The Society with which we are dealing in the two manifestoes is only a literary myth, but we can probably consider that the multiplication of initiatic societies starting in the eighteenth century finds one of its direct origins there (chapter 3, section III). Furthermore, the Rosicrucian current largely contributed to favor the interest of the period for speculations of a theosophical character related to Nature, in the Paracelsian wake. This interest was shared, notably, by Aegidius Gutman (*Offenbahrung göttlicher Majesteit*; published in 1619, this work had circulated since its completion, probably as early as 1575); by Simon Studion (whose *Naometria* of the same period, although still unpublished, was also in circulation); and by Johann Arndt (1555–1621).

In his *Vier Bücher vom wahren Christenthum* (principally in the last of the four volumes, published in 1610), Arndt develops and specifies what, beginning with him, would be called—in his own terms—"mystical theology." The latter was an attempt to integrate medieval mysticism, the neo-Paracelsian heritage, and alchemy, with theology—an integration possibly due, according to him, to a faculty attributed to the individual to achieve a "second birth," understood as the acquisition of a new body in the elected soul. It might seem permissible to see in this mystical theology a subtle link between the

Rosicrucian manifestoes and the *Chemical Wedding* of Andreae, but also one of the reasons for the vogue of the theosophical current.

III. Readings of the World and of Myths

1. *Philosophia Occulta*

From the end of the fifteenth century to that of the seventeenth, the currents hitherto mentioned all more or less belong to the so-called *philosophia occulta*, understood as a "magical" conception of the world where everything acts upon and reflects everything else analogically. Witchcraft and its spells, black magic, pacts with the Devil, and goety (*goetia*, invocation of angels or demons) are only very indirectly connected with these currents, but they represent like the dark side of this *philosophia occulta* and constitute an important sector of the *imaginaire* of those days.

Magia naturalis is a premodern form of natural science; it is the knowledge and the use of forces and occult virtues (powers) considered as "natural" because objectively present in nature (cf. e.g., *Magiae naturalis libri viginti*, 1589, of Giovanni Battista della Porta). It is hardly distinguishable from an experimental science still in its infancy and it often appears as a form of naturalism tainted with atheism. However, this ambiguous expression can also refer to a *magia* understood as an attempt to unify Nature and religion. To this *magia* belongs white magic or theurgy, which uses names, rites, and incantations with a view to establishing a personal link with entities not belonging to the world of physical creation. The two aspects of *magia naturalis* (the naturalist type, and white magic) are sometimes combined; thus, in "celestial" or "astronomical" magic, the stars are considered from a double viewpoint: as much their physical and natural influence as their "will" (cf. e.g., *De Vita coelitus comparanda*, 1489, by Ficino; *De occulta philosophia*, 1533, by Agrippa; section I, 1).

To these very representative names of "occult philosophy" let us add six of the principle ones (Fludd, Paracelsus; a number of others, cited *supra*, are obviously connected with it). Johannes Trithemius (1462–1516), abbot of Spanhein, is the author of a *Steganographia* that remained unpublished until 1606, and his *De Septem Secundeis* (1522) treats of the seven angels or intelligences animating the celestial orbs and the history of the world. Jacques Gohory (*alias* Leo Suavius, 1520–1576), musicologist, neo-Paracelsian, has left notably a *De usu et mysteriis notarum liber* (1550). To invoke the angels, the Elizabethan magus John Dee (1527–1609; section I, 1) combined Kabbalistic operations with the angelic hierarchies of Pseudo-Dionysius (*A True and Faithful Relation*, published in 1659). The Dominican Tommaso Campanella (1568–1639) is one of the last great philosophers of the Renaissance in the Ficinian tradition (*De sensu rerum et magia*, 1620). To these names should be added, of course, those of Francis Bacon (1561–1626; *Novum Organum*, 1620; *Sylva silvarum*, 1627); and Giordano Bruno (1548–1600; section I, 1), a Copernican marked by Alexandrian Hermetism and champion of a religious irenicism. In his occult philosophy of Nature, Bruno makes little room for the angelic world; and it was not his books of magic (*Sigillus sigillorum*, 1583; *De Imaginum . . . compositione*, 1591, etc.) that got him burned at the stake of the Inquisition, but rather his anti-Trinitarian and cosmological views (of an infinite universe, notably).

A celestial arithmetic and music is constant underpinning to these forms of "universal magic." Henceforth, and more than ever, astrology would take on the role of "queen of sciences." It lends itself well to this in its Paracelsian aspect, but in the seventeenth century, it also tended to assume a different one. The two famous theoreticians Placido Titi (*Physiomathematica*, 1650) and Jean-Baptiste Morin (*Astrologia Gallica*, 1661) aimed to tie it to the cosmologies of Aristotle and Ptolemy, at the very time when these cosmologies were definitively undermined by the discoveries in astronomy and by the new celestial mechanics. It nonetheless remains that in the sixteenth and the seventeenth centuries intermediary spirits, stars, and things of our Earth continued to "correspond" in the sense of interconnections that Ficino, for example, saw as occurring via the *spiritus mundi*, a vehicle of stellar influx. It is not the world of the medieval *Picatrix* that was changed; it is instead the role of humanity that was perceived differently, as less passive.

The main faculty—essentially "active"—that permits penetrating the world of correspondences is, as we have seen, the imagination—

the *vis imaginativa*—supposed to produce effects on our own body as on the outside of the latter, at the same time as it is an instrument of knowledge, of *gnosis*. Connected to this idea was the famous "Art of memory" inherited from procedures of medieval mnemotechnique and inspired by Alexandrian Hermetism. It consists in making enter, in some manner, into our mind—into our *mens*—human history, Nature, and all available knowledge, by associating mental images with mythological and planetary referents (cf. especially Giulio Camillo, *L'idea del teatro*, 1550, and various writings of Bruno and Fludd).

The arithmology of the neo-Pythagorean tradition made its presence felt in this whole in a manner that was usually obvious. It was the subject of specific treatment by Josse Clichtove (*De mystica numerorum significationae*, 1513), a disciple of Lefèvre d'Étaples around whom the arithmosophers Charles de Bovelles and Germain de Ganay also worked—or by Petrus Bungus (*Numerorum mysteria*, 1588). It was present in the cosmology of Johannes Kepler himself (*Mysterium cosmographicum*, 1596; section I, 1), who was also an astrologer. Numbers and mathematics were for Robert Fludd (*Utriusque cosmic historia*, 1617–1619; section III, 3) a privileged tool enabling study of the entire structure of the visible and invisible universe in its unity. He associated them intimately with music, just as Francesco Giorgi (section I, 1, 2) before him and Fabio Paolini (*Hebdomades*, 1589), or again Michael Maier in his *Atalanta fugiens* (1618; section III, 3).

The sixteenth century also witnessed the appearance of historical figures that posterity would cloak with an aura of mystery. Thus, Michel de Nostre-Dame (*alias* Nostradamus, 1503–1566), who practiced theurgy and wrote "prognostications" in verses, which relate to future history (his *Centuries* and his *Prophecies* have gone through a great number of re-editions.) In addition, Georg Faust, who lived from 1480 to about 1540, would have signed a pact with the Devil. Faust's sulfurous adventure was recounted in a German *Volksbuch* printed in 1587 (it has inspired countless works of fiction). Let us note finally that, in the form of *dissertationes* and *disputationes*, the universities of the seventeenth century, in Germany perhaps still more than elsewhere, bear witness to a lively interest in the occult. Moreover, in Spain and in Portugal a strong Islamic stamp created fertile ground for interest in *philosophia occulta*. To wit, *De Medendis corporis malis*

(1605), by Bravo Chamisso, a medical doctor from Louvain; and *Demonologia sive de magia*, (1623), by Francisco Torreblanca, a jurist from Cordova.

2. Alchemy: Science of Humanity, Nature, and Myths

Still at the beginning of the sixteenth century, the alchemical writings circulated mainly in manuscript form; thus, a treatise of Lodovico Lazzarelli (section I, 1), or the *De Auro* of Gianfrancesco Pico della Mirandola (written in 1527, published in 1586). Among the most widely known of the printed publications are the poem *Chrisopoeia* (1515) by G. A. Augurello, *Ars transmutationis* (1518) by J. A. Pantheus, and *Coelum philosophorum* (1525) by Philip Ulstad. To these works are added several anthologies of various treatises, such as *De Alchemia* in 1541 (which contains the first printed version of the famous text *The Emerald Tablet*), or *Verae alchemiae* . . . (1561) edited by Gulielmo Gratarolo.

Starting from the end of the century, an important part of alchemical literature fits into the Paracelsian wake and often appears as a proto-theosophy, as with Dorn and Khunrath (section II, 2). It further makes itself distinctly theosophizing in the case of Thomas Vaughan (*Magia adamica*, 1650). In England, Elias Ashmole, one of the founders of the Royal Society, contributed to its influence, and it was the purpose of the "Invisible College" of Samuel Hartlib to bring together all chemical and alchemical knowledge.

Besides this pansophic tendency, let us note three characteristic traits of seventeenth-century alchemy:

1. An interest in mythology, considered as a system of keys hiding the secrets of the Great Work under allegories (thus, in the case of Clovis Hesteau de Nuysement, *Traictez du vray Sel*, 1621; or Willem Mennens, *Aurei Velleris libri tres*, 1604). This tendency goes back to the High Middle Ages.

2. A taste for fine illustrations (*infra*, 3).

3. Editions of encyclopedias, anthologies, and sometimes voluminous compilations: *Theatrum Chemicum*, 1602 (edited by Eberhard Zetzner) several re-editions, including the one in six large volumes (1659–1661); *Theatrum Chemicum Britannicum*, introduced by Elias

Ashmole, 1652; *Musaeum Hermeticum*, 1678; *Bibliotheca chemica curiosa*, edited by Jean-Jacques Manget (1702, 2 in-fol.).

Alchemy was patronized by German emperors (Rudolf II of Prague especially, but also Ferdinand II) and many princes, because they thought of gaining riches through the transmutations of metals. Some of the learned founders of modern science did not disdain it. Isaac Newton devoted a considerable time to it (most of the many alchemical writings that he has left date from the seven or eight years that followed the appearance of his *Principia* of 1686). Finally, we could not overemphasize that, in a general manner over the course of this long period, the alchemists clearly strove to do "scientific" work and not—contrary to what is too easily believed today—to oppose who knows what "official science" of their time.

3. A Hermetico-Emblematic Art

A hermeticizing art is present in Renaissance Italy. Either a character like the Trismegistus himself appears in the figures (thus, in 1488, on the pavement of the cathedral of Sienna), or zodiacal signs, mythical characters and hermetic symbols are associated to create frescoes or paintings (Borgia apartments in the Vatican, the *Primavera* of Botticelli in 1478, etc). With the first plates of his *De Mundi aetatibus imagines* (1545–1573), the Portuguese Francesco de Holanda proved himself a brilliant precursor of Jacob Boehme and of William Blake.

From the end of the sixteenth century and for about thirty years, we see the flowering of many works in which the importance of the engravings is equal to or greater than that of the text itself. Mostly alchemical, the engravings are in the line of the emblematic tradition born with Andrea Alciati's *Emblemata* (1551). These include, for example, *Cabala* (1616) of Stephan Michelspacher, *Opus medicochymicus* and *Philosophia reformata* (1622) of J. D. Mylius, *De lapide philosophico* of Lampsprinck (1625), the anthology of Ashmole (*supra*, 2), the *Mutus liber* (1677, without text) or again the celebrated *Atalanta fugiens* (1618, section III, 1) of Michael Maier, in which each of the fifty emblematic plates is accompanied by a text and a musical score. Not essentially alchemical but instead theosophical are certain works that are admirably illustrated, such as the *Amphitheatrum Sapientiae Aeternae* (section II, 2; section III, 2) of Heinrich Khunrath, the *Utriusque Cosmi historia* (1617–1621) of Robert Fludd—or again the almost complete edition (1682) of Boehme's works, in Amsterdam, presented by Johann Georg Gichtel (section II, 2).

Literature, too, also maintained fruitful relationships with esotericism. The *Hypnerotomachia* (or *Dream of Poliphile*, 1499) by Francesco Colonna, the *Cinquième Livre* (1564) by François Rabelais, and the *Voyage des Princes fortunés* (1610) by Beroalde de Verville belong to a "literary esotericism" in some ways comparable to that of Andreae's Rosicrucian novel (1616; section II, 3). Mannerism and occult sciences got along harmoniously in the works of Maurice Scève (*Microcosme*, 1562), Guy Lefèvre de la Boderie (*La Gaillade*, 1578), Fabio Paolini (*Hebdomades*, 1589; section II, 2), Edmund Spencer (*The Fairie Queene*, 1596), Torquato Tasso (*Mondo creato*, 1607), and Giambattista Marino (*Dicerie Sacre*, 1614). Dramatists brought this same science onto the Elizabethan stage, whether their plays are permeated with it (William Shakespeare, *The Tempest*, 1610) or are concerned with mocking it (Ben Jonson, *The Alchemist*, 1610). But such works are countless, from the baroque and theosophical collection of poems *Cherubinischer Wandersmann* (1675) of Johann Scheffler (*alias* Angelus Silesius) to the explicitly alchemical theater of Christian Knorr von Rosenroth (*Conjugium Phoebis et Palladis*, 1677), and including the very popular *Comte de Gabalis ou entretiens sur les sciences secrètes* (1670) of Montfaucon de Villars.

The paintings of Jerome Bosch ("The Garden of Delights," toward 1510) and of Peter Breughel the elder (*Dulle Griet*, 1562) have not yet revealed all their mysteries. Two pictorial works of the seventeenth century merit particular attention. One is the anonymous painting *La Vierge alchimique*, visible in the Saint-Rémy Museum of Reims, of Hermetist and arithmosophical connotations, a work probably sponsored by the Jesuits and dating from the beginning of the seventeenth century. The other is the Kabbalistic altarpiece *Turris Antonia* (or "didactic tablet of the princess Antonia de Wurtemberg"), painted at Bad Teinach, near Stuttgart (1663–1673). Both are still located in their place of origin. The examples are many. For instance, one of the engravings of the *Icones Biblicae* of Matthieu Merian (reproduced in the Lutheran Bible of Strasbourg, 1623) represents the Wedding at Cana in a setting that seems to allude to both the Rosicrucian teachings and the alchemical transmutation.

3

Esotericism in the Shadow of the Enlightenment

I. Sunburst of Theosophy

1. At the Dawn of Illuminism

Translated into German in 1706 (with a Paracelsian commentary), the *Corpus Hermeticum* (CH) also was the subject of scholarly presentations in late Germanic humanism (*Bibliotheca Graeca* of J. A. Fabricius, 1708–1727). However, it also had recently been the subject, along with the neo-Alexandrian current, Rosicrucianism, and theosophy, of a refutation by Daniel Ehregott Colberg, a Lutheran theologian. His voluminous work *Das platonisch-hermetisches [sic] Christenthum* (1690–1691), as hostile as it may have been, nevertheless represents the first "history" ever written of the modern esoteric currents (until the end of the seventeenth century). It was soon followed by a monumental work by Gottfried Arnold, a theosopher and sophiologist (chapter 2, section II, 2), who devoted a copious historical work to them (and to a good number of "mystical" authors) (*Unpartheyische Kirchen- und Ketzerhistorie*, 1699–1700). A little later came long and very critical developments by Jacob Brucker, a Protestant historian of philosophy, on Kabbalah, Pythagoreanism, and theosophy, in his *Historia critica philosophiae* (vols. II and IV, 1743)—a compendium widely read throughout the time of the Enlightenment and even later.

In England, in the 1720s, Dionysius Andreas Freher wrote many commentaries on the works of Boehme (they would remain unpublished but would circulate in various milieux open to receiving them), and William Law (*The Way to Divine Knowledge*, 1752) contributed to the continuity of the theosophical current. In Switzerland, the famous "Berleburg Bible" (1726–1742) also made a contribution, by introducing it into the pietist milieux. It was again at Berleburg that Hector de Saint-Georges de Marsais published his works (such as *Explication de la Genèse*, 1738), influenced—as much as this Bible is—by Boehme, Mme Guyon, and Pierre Poiret. *Le Mystère de la Croix* (1732), a work signed by Douzetemps, is an example of an interpenetration of mysticism, pietism, and theosophy.

On the edge of this tendency orientated toward a certain form of "mysticism" another one appeared, by which the initiatic societies of the second half of the eighteenth century would draw inspiration, and which lies in a more Paracelsian wake. It is represented especially by three major works of a theosophical type, written in German and reprinted several times. These are, first, *Theo-Philosophia Theoretico practica* (1711) by Samuel Richter (*alias* Sincerus Renatus); second, *Aurea catena Homeri* (1723) by A. J. Kirchweger; and third, *Opus mago cabbalisticum et theosophicum* (1719) by Georg von Welling (*alias* Salwigt), a book that would long be deeply influential—not least on the young Johann Wolfgang Goethe.

Freemasonry as it is usually understood (i.e., "speculative Freemasonry"), appeared in London in 1717. Toward 1730, it introduced into its rituals the myth of the death and the resurrection of Hiram. This would favor the appearance—but essentially on the continent—starting from the 1750s, of masonic or paramasonic Rites (also sometimes called Systems, or Orders) with Higher Grades (or "Degrees"), that is, above the three grades of Entered Apprentice, Fellow Craft, and Master Mason, which constitute what is called "blue" or Craft Masonry. The creators of certain neo-Rosicrucian Higher Grades in the second half of the century drew upon the three works in German above (see also section III, 1, 2).

2. The Great Theosophers

The years from 1770 to about 1815 correspond to what it is commonly called the period of Illuminism (section I, 3). Theosophy then shone again in all its brilliance.

The Swede Emanuel Swedenborg (1688–1772), a reputed scientist, interrupted his properly scientific activities in 1745 following dreams that had suddenly come to transform his inner life. He immersed himself then in the study of the Bible and wrote his *Arcana coelestia* (1747–1758), followed by many other works.

Swedenborg presented his visions using images and figures that constitute a type of descriptive, even realistic, geography of the celestial spheres, of the "spiritual" worlds. His work greatly contributed to disseminate to a wide audience the idea of universal correspondences that, from Nature to humanity and from humanity to God, appear as an indefinite series of intermediaries. In the natural world, any object, even the most minor, "corresponds" to something that partakes of a higher order of reality, without solution of continuity. A sometimes colorful but generally rather flat style is off-putting to many readers, but the fame of this visionary spread quickly as early as the 1770s, notably by means of many translations and abridgements. They penetrated into various intellectual milieux. Immanuel Kant devoted a whole treatise to Swedenborg (*Träume eines Geistersehers*, 1766; translated as *Dreams of a Spirit Seer*). Moreover, no theosopher has exerted a more significant influence on literature than he has. Most of the other great theosophers did not value Swedenborg highly, whose Christology appeared suspicious to them and whose cosmology left little room for Nature. However, "Swedenborgianism" inspired some masonic Rites and, in 1787, even incited Anglican ecclesiastics to create a little Church, the New Church, still flourishing today.

The Swabian Friedrich Christoph Oetinger (1702–1782; section II, 3), Lutheran pastor, Nature philosopher, and alchemist, nourished by Boehme and the Kabbalah, exegete of Swedenborg from whom he nevertheless strongly distanced himself, represents a form of eclectic and erudite esotericism. *Magia*, the highest of sciences, is for him a method of knowledge in the search for connections between terrestrial and celestial physics. Everything, for him, is "physical"—however "subtle" it may be. There are no such things as pure spirits ("Corporeality is the end [the goal] of the works of God," was one of his mottos). To practice a "superior physics" and a permanent hermeneutic (nourished by Kabbalah and alchemy) can furnish us with keys to knowledege about the relationships between Nature and the Bible.

Among his principal works appeared *Biblisches und emblematisches Wörterbuch* (1776), and *Oeffentliches Denckmal der Princessen Antonia* (1763; the latter consists of a commentary on the *Turris Antonia*, cf. chapter 2, section III, 3). Through an essay on the Kabbalah of Isaac Luria (chapter 2, section I, 2), Oetinger contributed to make known to the German pietists the Hassidism that is spiritually so close to pietism.

Less a physicist and less a Kabbalist, Michael Hahn (1758–1819) is, however, a great theosopher in the lineage of Boehme. His writings on androgyny and the Sophia remain classics of the genre. More cele-brated, more popular by his writings, only little influenced by Boehme, is Karl von Eckartshausen (1752–1803; section III, 3), of Munich. His work (which includes *Zahlenlehre der Natur* [1794] and the famous *Die Wolke über dem Heiligthum*—1802, translated as *The Cloud upon the Sanctuary*) is exceedingly rich. His major books, translated and republished in several languages (many in Russian, notably), have to date never ceased to find a hearing. It is also in German that the Alsa-tian Frédéric R. Saltzmann wrote, in the first years of the nineteenth century, a theosophical work in the Boehmean wake, but with a more limited reception (*Es wird alles neu werden*, 1802–1810).

The *Traité de la Réintégration des êtres*, by Martines de Pasqually (1727–1774; section III, 1)—the founder of the theurgical Order of the Élus-Coëns—is one of the masterpieces of modern theosophy. Under its influence, Louis-Claude de Saint-Martin (1743–1803; chapter 4, section I, 2), who would call himself "the Unknown Philosopher," composed his first two works, *Des Erreurs et de la vérité* (1775) and *Tableau naturel des rapports qui existent entre Dieu, l'homme et l'univers* (1781). During a sojourn in Strasbourg (1788–1791), he befriended Frédéric R. Saltzmann (cf. *supra*) who had him discover Boehme. Henceforth strongly under Boehme's spell, he produced other master works of theosophy, including *L'Homme de désir* (1790), *Le Nouvel homme* and *Ecce Homo* (1792), *Le Ministère de l'Homme-Esprit* and *De l'Esprit des choses* (1802).

Saint-Martin was not simply an emulator of Pasqually and of Boehme, but was especially the most important theosopher of his time as well as one of the principal representatives of preromantic literature in France. His influence, as much direct as diffuse, has never ceased to make itself felt. He has left behind interesting correspondence with masons or Élus-Coëns such as Jean-Baptiste Willermoz (1730–1824; section II, 3; section III, 1), as well as with personalities spiritually still closer to him, such as the Bernese Niklaus Anton Kirchberger (1739–1799).

In this gallery of famous theosophers, another Swiss has his place, Jean-Philippe Dutoit-Membrini (1721–1793), author of a *Philosophie divine* (1793) that also appears among the important works produced by this current. Finally, the last years of the century and the period of the Empire saw the emergence, especially in Germany, of a Nature philosophy (a *Naturphilosophie*) often strongly tinged with theosophy (*infra*, section III).

3. Faces of Illuminism

As recalled earlier, *Illuminism* is the term used to refer to a general orientation of thought that flourished from the 1760s to the beginning of the nineteenth century. If it is especially represented by the theosophers, it is also by all those who found themselves more or less in affinity with them, and by a number of initiatic societies (*infra*, section III). Accordingly, won over generally to theosophy but marked by forms of devotional esotericism or notable singularities as well, various characters compose this gallery.

First is the engaging Johann Caspar Lavater (1741–1801). A Lutheran minister in Zurich, curious about supernatural phenomena, he did not scorn theurgy, practiced animal magnetism occasionally, and developed ideas impregnated with a form of naturalistic Christology (*Aussichten in die Ewigkeit*, 1768–1778), but posterity sees in him especially the first great modern theoretician of physiognomy (*Physiognomische Fragmente*, 1775–1778). Probably few German-speaking thinkers since Luther maintained a correspondence as monumental as his.

Johann Heinrich Jung-Stilling (1740–1817; section III, 3) resembled him by the magnitude of his correspondence and his researches in "metapsychical" phenomena (*Theorie der Geisterkunde*, 1807). Communications with the spirit world were also a focal point for Jean Frederic Oberlin (1740–1826), a Protestant minister in Steinthal (Alsace). In

Russia, Ivan Vladimirovich Lopukhin (1775–1815; section III, 1) has left a short work that met with long-standing success: *Quelques traits de l'Église intérieure* (Some Characteristics of the Interior Church), written in Russian in 1791, published in French in 1798, several times translated and republished, close to Hesychasm by the techniques of prayer that are taught in it. This prominent figure of Russian Freemasonry translated into his language, and published, texts by Boehme, Swedenborg, Eckartshausen, and Jung-Stilling.

Besides these avenues of Christian spirituality, Illuminism included other figures, of a neo-pagan orientation. If Antoine Fabre d'Olivet wrote *La Langue hebraïque restituée* (1810, published in 1816–1817; section II, 4), it was not by Christian zeal but rather by a concern to discover the origin of language. His *Vers dorés de Pythagore* (1813) attempt to demonstrate the existence of a lost but universal Tradition. Less philosophical, and mainly encyclopedic, is the great survey realized by Antoine Court de Gébelin, *Le Monde primitif* (1773–1784), one of the first attempts to find, through the exploration of various known traditions, something that resembles what would later be called the "primordial Tradition" (chapter 5, section II, 1, 2). Moreover, the egyptophilian trend of that time inspired many discourses and practices replete with initiatic frameworks—from the novel by Abbot Terrasson (*Sethos*, 1731) to *Nouvelles recherches sur l'origine et la destination des pyramides d'Egypte* (1812) by A. P. J. de Vismes, including "Egyptian Masonries" (section III, 2) like *The Magic Flute* (Mozart's opera, 1791) and *Kostis Reise* (1795, a short novel by Eckartshausen).

II. From the Art of Reading to the Art of Subtle Fluids

I. Continuity of the Occult Sciences

Thanks to some learned treatises, interest in Christian Kabbalah had not yet entirely abated in the second half of the century. Thus, initiated by the Christian Kabbalist Christian Fende and by the Jewish Kabbalist Koppel Hecht, Oetinger (section I, 2) wrote his famous *Lehrtafel* ("Didactic tablet," 1763), an interpretation of an altarpiece painted in the preceding century and conserved in the church of

Bad Teinach (chapter 2, section III, 3). Pythagoreanism and Hermetism pursued their virtually uninterrupted course (to wit, many neo-Pythagorean writings, such as *Les Voyages de Pythagore en Egypte*, by Sylvain Maréchal, 1799; and a new German translation of the *Pimander*, 1781).

In the less learned context of the salons and the street corners, the era of Illuminism was hospitable to the career of characters expert in exploiting the taste for the marvelous, such as the Count of Saint Germain (?–1784) and Joseph Balsamo (*alias* Cagliostro (1743 [?]–1795; section II, 2). The powers that credulous contemporaries attributed to them reflect a general taste for the so-called occult sciences, as witnessed notably by the editions of books of popular magic (like the *Grand Albert* and the *Petit Albert*), by heated debates on vampirism (especially from 1732 to the *Traité sur les apparitions* [1746] of Dom Calmet), and witchcraft. Noteworthy too is the widespread interest evinced at that time for automata and entertaining experiments in physics.

An engaging and disconcerting character incarnates rather well the different forms of this state of mind on the eve of the Revolution. This was the Frenchman Jean-Baptiste Alliette (*alias* Etteilla), a combination of charlatan and theosopher, and an alchemist as well (*Les Sept Nuances de l'oeuvre philosophique*, 1786). One of his claims to glory is to have been practically the first to spread the idea that the Tarot cards, so-called of Marseille, would go back to ancient Egypt and would contain sublime mysteries. A little later, more in the wake of Agrippa's *De Occulta philosophia* (chapter 2, section I, 1; chapter 2, section III, 1), a compilation destined for great success prefigures the editorial production of the occultist current that would flourish starting in the middle of the nineteenth century. This is *The Magus* (1801), by Francis Barrett (besides whom we may also cite Karl Joseph Windischmann, author of *Untersuchungen über Astrologie, Alchemie und Magie*, 1813).

Music was the subject of esoteric speculations, not least with regard to synesthesia: an ocular (color-liquid) clavichord or "color piano" (it displayed colors supposed to be in harmony with the notes) was described notably by the Jesuit Louis-Bertrand Castel around 1740—and later more extensively by Eckartshausen (section I, 2;

section III, 3) in his *Aufschlüsse zur Magie* (1788). But Saint-Martin (section I, 2) was perhaps the only one of the century to integrate perfectly an elaborate speculation about music into a theosophical discourse (especially in *Des Erreurs et de la Vérité*, 1775, and *De l'Esprit des choses*, 1802). However, A. P. J. de Vismes also appeared on this terrain (*Essai sur l'homme, ou l'homme microcosme*, 1805) and Fabre d'Olivet, with his first researches (section I, 3). Finally, it was a period of intense activity for illuminated prophets: Suzette Labrousse and Catherine Théot in revolutionary France; on the eve of the Empire, Mademoiselle Lenormand; in England, Richard Brothers; in Germany, Thomas Poeschl—and many others a bit everywhere.

2. Alchemy, Shadow Side of the Enlightenment and Light of Mythology

The progress of chemistry, which definitively acquired its status of a scientific discipline, already heralded the irremediable decline of operative alchemy. However, interest remained lively and the litera-ture abundant, even after the publication of the works of Lavoisier. In the *Encyclopedia* of Diderot, the articles "Alchemy" and "Alchemist" by Maloin were not testimony to hostility toward this "science." This is because scholars believed to read in it a poorly explored area of investigation. The common people saw in it a source of immediate wealth, the unconditional rationalists a practice of charlatans, and for part of the public it was an aspect among others of the marvelous. This concerned especially the manufacturing of material gold (the alchemy called "operative"), but, as in the preceding periods, it is not always easy to distinguish "operative" and "spiritual" alchemy—the latter, as we have seen, often being considered as a form of sublime knowledge. From a still considerable editorial production (but from which the tradition of fine illustrations had unfortunately disappeared), let us highlight three aspects of which the first two were situated in the extension of what we have mentioned *supra* (chapter 2, section III, 2), but took renewed forms.

The first aspect is illustrated by the vogue that the compilations of treatises continued to enjoy. Whereas the anthology of Jean-Jacques Manget (chapter 3, section III, 2) was in Latin, there now appeared, in the vernacular, the *Deutsches Theatrum Chemicum* (1728) of Friedrich Roth-Scholtz, the *Neue Alchymistische Bibliothek* (1772) of F. J. W. Schröder, and others like them. As a corollary, there was a public demand for historiographical presentations: hence the publication of works such as the *Bibliotheca chemica* (1727) of Roth-Scholtz, the *Histoire de la philosophie hermétique* (1742) of Nicolas Lenglet-Dufresnoy, and the *Dictionnaire mytho-hermétique* (1758) of the Benedictine Antoine Joseph Pernety (section III, 2).

The second aspect is characterized (as previously, chapter 2, section III, 2) by the tendency to give stories of Greek and Egyptian mythology an alchemical reading. This was achieved by reducing the antique "Fables" to an allegorical discourse, whose sole purpose would have been the encrypted description of procedures of transmutation (typical in this regard are the *Fables égyptiennes et grecques dévoilées*, 1758, by Antoine Dom Pernety). Alternatively, it was accomplished by interpreting this mythology on several levels, in a nonreductionist manner, following a hermeneutic of a theosophical type (thus proceeded Hermann Fictuld, *Aureum Vellus*, 1749; Ehrd de Naxagoras, *Aureum Vellus*, 1753, both in German; or again Anselmo Caetano, *Ennoea*, 1732–1733, in Portuguese).

The third aspect of alchemy at the time of the Enlightenment was its diffuse but obvious presence among scientists and Nature philosophers more or less won over to Paracelsism such as Johann Juncker (*Conspectus chemiae theoretico-practicae*, 1730) and, later of course, Oetinger. This characteristic prefigured Romantic *Naturphilosophie* (section IV, 1, 2).

3. Animal Magnetism

According to one of the most widespread ideas in alchemical thought, matter contains a light or an invisible fire whose nature is that of the Word who created Light on the first Day. This igneous principle, halfway between the natural and the supersensible, also occupies an important place in many cosmological discourses of the West. It has served to interpret the Platonic idea of the World Soul and has diversified into countless themes and motifs. Spread in the eighteenth century, the tendency to mix experimental research and speculative thought favored the reappearance of this principle under new forms. In the seventeenth century, Rudolf Göckel and Athanasius Kircher (chapter 2, section I, 1) were passionately interested in phenomena of a magnetic and electric nature.

At the time of the Enlightenment, some Nature philosophers close to Oetinger (section I, 2) developed a "theology of electricity." These were especially J. L. Fricker, G. F. Rösler, Prokop Divisch (*Theorie der meterologischen Elektrizität*, 1765). Their speculations were clad in a light of religiosity, but those of the Swabian doctor Franz Anton Mesmer (1734–1815) were not—he was a materialist. Mesmerism, however, soon became a source of inspiration to most of the representatives of the esoteric currents of that time.

As early as 1766, in his doctoral thesis, *De influx planetarum in corpus humanum*, Mesmer had postulated the existence of an invisible fluid spread everywhere. It would serve as a vehicle for the mutual influence that the celestial bodies would exert between themselves, the Earth and animate bodies—whence the expression "animal magnetism" generally employed to refer to this theory and the practices connected with it. Having first cared for his patients by the application of magnets (a procedure later readopted by Jean-Martin Charcot), then by the laying on of hands, he developed a therapy that consisted in having people sit next to one another around a tub—the famous *baquet*—containing water, iron filings, and sand. They communicated with the tub by means of iron rods or ropes and thus formed a "chain" in order to transmit into the bodies of the sick patients the "magnetism" of the healthy subjects. Established in Paris in 1778, Mesmer enjoyed great success there but also came up against the incomprehension of official medicine. Nicolas Bergasse attempted to develop a doctrine of magnetism (*Théorie du monde et des êtres organisés*, 1784) that was to prove influential for many decades.

Although a convinced materialist, Mesmer himself gave his activities an "initiatic" character by creating in 1783 a Society of Harmony of which a number of symbols were inspired by the masonic style. And, in 1785, he wrote that "we are endowed with an internal sense that is in relationship with the whole of the entire universe"—an idea that would not fail to create many repercussions in the currents we are dealing with. This was all the more so as the notion of "internal sense," widespread in that period, assumed different meanings there. Whereas according to Kant this notion resembles an impoverishment, in the case of Mesmer it can signify on the contrary a deployment of the possibilities of our being. Anyhow, far from spreading in the specific form that Mesmer had attempted to confer on it, animal magnetism could soon be seen operating in several directions.

Notably, whereas Mesmer had conceived the practice for an essentially therapeutic purpose, as early as 1784, in France, the Marquis Armand Marie Jacques de Chastenet de Puységur (1727–1807), who "magnetized" his subjects by sending them into a state of consciousness close to sleep, believed he had discovered the possibility of nonverbal control exercised on them by the magnetizer. He was one of the first to consider the material supports used by Mesmer (such as magnets, tubs, etc.) as nonessential. He was also among the first, in the history of animal magnetism, to attempt to show that a magnetized person can sometimes be capable of "clairvoyance," that is, seeing objects that are hidden or situated in distant places, predicting things in the future, diagnosing illnesses and indicating their remedies, and so on. Thus, open to the "paranormal," animal magnetism could even be considered by many as a means to establish contacts with the beyond; for example, by Jean-Baptiste Willermoz, in Lyons, and by some of the principal representatives of *Naturphilosophie* in Germany (chapter 4, section I, 3). Let us also recall that animal magnetism was not merely a fashion or an isolated episode, but represented a most important cultural trend at the twilight of the Enlightenment, in romantic thought in the broad sense, and in the history of dynamic psychiatry until the time of Sigmund Freud inclusively.

III. A Century of Initiations

1. Strict Observance and Rectified Scottish Rite

Much more than the first three Grades (Entered Apprentice, Fellow Craft, Master Mason) of Freemasonry, it was, we have seen (chapter

3, section I, 1), the Higher Grades of certain Rites that drew from the thematic corpus of the esoteric currents. Before reviewing the principle ones of these Rites, let us first introduce two of the most famous. The first, called Strict Observance (SO), created by the Baron Karl von Hund toward 1750, presented itself as a direct descendant (so at least it claimed to be) of the Order of the Temple destroyed by Philip IV the Fair. SO remained the most important masonic Rite in Germany for about thirty years. The second was the Rectified Scottish Rite (RER), which included the so-called Order of the Knights Beneficient of the Holy City (Chevaliers Bienfasants de la Cité Sainte [CBCS])—from the name of the sixth grade of the RER. This Rite, whose principal architect was the theosopher from Lyons Jean-Baptiste Willermoz (section I, 2; section III, 1), was not of a theurgic character although it was inspired from the Order of the Élus-Coëns founded in France some time around 1754 by the theosopher Martines de Pasqually (chapter 3, section I, 2).

At the end of the 1770s, two of the principal personalities of the SO, Duke Ferdinand von Brunswick and Prince Karl von Hessen-Cassel, decided to assemble the representatives of European Freemasonry in a great Masonic Convention responsible for reflecting on the origin, the nature, the reason for being of this institution. With this in mind, Ferdinand sent out circulars to various personalities (Joseph de Maistre, initiated into the RER, responded with his famous *Mémoire* of 1780). The Convention met at Wilhelmsbad in July–August 1782. There, the myth of Templar filiation was discarded, and the orientation represented by the RER became an object of global acceptance.

This Convention was an important event of the era because we can see two categories of Masons confronted there. Some were attracted to various forms of "esotericism"; others instead staunchly adhered to the philosophy of the Enlightenment. Under the name "Martinism" (from the names of Saint-Martin and de Pasqually), the RER quickly gained footing in Russia where the Golden Rosy-Cross (*infra*, 2) had also penetrated and where the masons Lopukhin (section I, 3) and Nicolay Ivanovich Novikov stood out as two of the principle representatives of this orientation.

2. Other Masonic and Paramasonic Systems

Let us distinguish between, on the one hand, the Christian Rites (of which SO and RER are part), of a medieval "chivalrous" type, having the Holy Land, Jerusalem, as their "Orient" of reference; and, on the other hand, the rather neo-pagan or "Egyptian" Rites. Between them, however, the frontier was fluid and, of course, the same person could appear simultaneously in several of these Rites. An Order that called itself "Rosicrucian," constituted in the 1770s in Germany, achieved the cohesion of its Lodges or "Circles" in 1777 by naming itself the Gold- und Rosenkreutzer Älteren Systems (Golden Rosicrucians of the Ancient System), and by endowing itself with nine grades very marked by alchemical symbolism. With the advent (1786) of the new King of Prussia Frederick William II, who had taken initiation into that Order, the latter entered into definitive dormancy without having been for as much forbidden. Its editorial activities constituted a non-negligible aspect of production of an esoteric type at the end of the century (cf. e.g., the *Geheime Figuren der Rosenkreuzer*, 1785–1788, a collection of plates and texts that would often be reproduced and interpreted).

Pernety (section II, 2) may have known Golden Rosicrucians in Berlin where he found himself from 1767 to 1782 in the position of curator of the Royal Library of Frederick II. He left this city in 1783, went to Avignon, established not far from there his (non-masonic) society known as the Illuminés d'Avignon, and engaged in oracular practices of interrogating a "Sainte Parole" ("Holy Word"), a sort of hypostasis of the Supreme Intelligence. The Polish staroste Thaddeus Leszczyc Grabianka, a member of this Society, created a dissident group in this city, called The New Israel, whose head was Ottavio Cappelli, a gardener believed to be receiving communications from the archangel Raphael. The revolutionary upheaval scattered the Illuminés d'Avignon, of which many personalities of Europe were part.

Let us cite eleven other initiatic societies of a Christian character. The Swedish Rite was established toward 1750 by Karl Friedrich Eckleff. The Ordre de l'Étoile Flamboyante was founded by Théodore Henri de Tschoudy (1766). The Rite of Johann Wilhelm Zinnendorf (1770) was inspired by the Swedish Rite. The Klerikat (Clericate) was the creation of Johann August Starck toward 1767. The Society of the Philalethes came to birth in 1773; this Society, which was probably the first institute of research into Freemasonry, had Charles Pierre Savalette de Langes among its foremost members. In Paris, in 1785 and 1787, it organized two international interobediential Conventions meant to put all the possible documents and archives in common with a view to discovering or rediscovering the true principles on which Freemasonry should rest. The Brethren of the Cross was a Rite founded by Christian Heinrich Haugwitz toward 1777. The Asiatic Brethren, in Austria and in south Germany especially, was the creation of Hans Heinrich von Ecker- und Eckhoffen in 1781. François Marie Chefdebien d'Armissan and his father founded The Primitive Rite of the Philadelphians in 1780. The Illuminated Theosophists, of Swedenborgian type, important in England and in the United States was a Rite born toward 1783 under the impetus of Benedict Chastanier. The Ancient and Accepted Scottish Rite (REAA) came to birth in France around 1801. The Order of the Orient was founded in 1804 and organized in 1806 by Bernard-Raymond Fabré-Palaprat, under the denomination of the Johannite Church of Primitive Christians, which is a neo-Templar organization. With the three systems cited in the preceding section (SO, Elect-Cohens, and RER), we count here fourteen of them.

As for the "neo-pagan" Rites, of "Egyptian" character for the most part, they were principally the five following: the African Architects, creation of Friedrich von Köppen toward 1767; the Egyptian Rite created by Cagliostro (section II, 1), which dates from 1784; at the beginning of the French Empire appeared in Italy the Rite of Misraïm (although not very "Egyptian" in character), which was imported into France by the Bédarride brothers, and followed in 1815 by the Rite of Memphis—to which it is fitting to add that of the so-called Magi of Memphis, created at the end of the eighteenth century and that refers explicitly to Hermes Trismegistus. But this list of nineteen Rites does not claim to be exhaustive.

3. Initiation in Art

The eighteenth century saw a proliferation of works of fiction replete with mysteries. Witnesses to this were first a French translation of the

Arabian Nights ("Les Mille et une Nuits") by Antoine Galand (1704), of re-editions and translations of the *Comte de Gabalis* (chapter 2, section III, 3), or again a collection of imposing dimensions such as the *Voyages imaginaires* (cf. notably volume XIV, *Relation du Monde de Mercure*). Then, fruitful relationships were sealed between eighteenth-century Illuminism and literature. In *Le Diable amoureux* (1772) of Jacques Cazotte (a well-known "Illuminé"), we can detect one of the direct origins of the specific type of writing that would flourish starting in the mid-nineteenth century and that would be known as the classical 'fantastic' genre in literature of fiction.

In the period of Illuminism, works of fiction were sometimes of a humorous (Mouhy, *Lamekis*, 1737) or parodic (F. H. von Hippel, *Kruez- und Querzüge*, 1793) bent, sometimes more serious—notably starting in the last ten years of the eighteenth century, especially in Germany; in which case it was illustrated by novelists such as Jean Paul (*Die Unsichtbare Loge*, 1793), Johann Heinrich Jung-Stilling (*Heimweh*, 1794; section I, 3), Eckartshausen (*Kostis Reise*, 1795; section I, 2), Saint-Martin (*Le Crocodile*, 1799), Novalis (*Heinrich von Ofterdingen* and *Die Lehrlinge zu Sais*, 1802), Ernst Theodor Amadeus Hoffmann (*Der golden Topf*, 1813), and even by Goethe (cf. the tale "Das Märchen," 1795 [translated into English under the title *The Green Snake and the Beautiful Lily*]; his poem "Das Geheimnisse," 1785; certain passages in *Faust Part One*).

The opera of Mozart *The Magic Flute* (1791) and the drama of Zacharias Werner *Die Söhne des Thals* (1802–1804) remain two of the most well known works in the performing arts. William Blake, poet, engraver, bard of the creative imagination (*The Marriage of Heaven and Earth*, 1793; *Visions of the Daughter of Albion*, 1793), transmuted contributions from many currents, among which Swedenborgism, in the alchemical furnace of his genius. We could cite many other authors in the English domain, such as James Thomson, of which *The Seasons* (1726–1730) revealed deep tinges of Hermetism. More than all the other painters of German romanticism, Philipp Otto Runge (chapter 2, section I, 5) was close to theosophy, especially to that of Boehme (cf. his painting of "Morning," 1808). Finally, in Italy, we owe Prince Raimondo di Sangro di San Severo, from whom Cagliostro received teachings, the astonishing "Hermetic monument" preserved in the San Severo Chapel in Naples.

4

From Romantic Knowledge to Occultist Programs

I. The Era of *Naturphilosophie* and the Great Syntheses

I. Nature Philosophy in the Romantic Era (1790–1847)

In the last decade of the eighteenth century, a new manner of approaching the study of Nature emerged, which lasted about fifty years and barely reappeared thereafter. This is *Naturphilosophie*, which is especially part of German romanticism in the broad sense. In several of its representatives, it takes an aspect that pairs it directly with the theosophical current. In its most general form, it is, as Friedrich W. J. von Schelling describes it, an attempt to bring to light that which Christianity had always repressed—namely, Nature. Three factors contributed to this dawning.

First is the persistence of the idea of *magia* among chemist-physicists such as Oetinger (chapter 3, section I, 2). The second factor is the influence exerted by certain philosophers: French naturalism (Georges-Louis de Buffon, Jean Le Rond d'Alembert), not lacking in speculations on the life of matter; Immanuel Kant, who appeared to see in the universe a product of the imagination, of the synthesizing and spontaneous activity of the mind; Baruch Spinoza, in whom people believed they then discovered that Nature is something spiritual and that the whole of the finite world proceeds from a Spirit, a focus of energy. The third factor is the atmosphere proper to the preromantic period, which has a taste for animal magnetism, galvanism, electricity (experiments of Galvani in 1789, Volta battery in 1800), and which sees the publication of bold syntheses developed by great *Kulturphiloso-phen* such as Johann Gottfried Herder. Now, three fundamental tenets seem to characterize *Naturphilosophie*:

1. *The "identity" of Spirit and Nature*, considered as the two seeds of a single common root. Nature rests on a spiritual principle: a Spirit inhabits it, speaks through it (a *natura naturans* is hidden behind the *natura naturata*), and she has a history: She is, like the Spirit, engaged in a process of a highly dramatic character.

2. *Nature is a living net of correspondences to be deciphered and integrated into a holistic worldview.* It is full of symbolic implications and its true meaning escapes merely empirical examination. Consequently, rigorous experimentation is never more than a necessary first step towards a comprehensive, holistic knowledge of both visible and invisible processes.

3. *Naturphilosophie is by definition multidisciplinary.* Its representatives are all more or less specialists (chemists, physicists, physicians, geologists, and engineers), but their thinking extends to eclectic syntheses striving to encompass, in its complexity, a polymorphous universe made of different degrees of reality. The compartmentalization of Nature into strictly distinct subjects here gives way to the attempt to grasp a Whole animated by dynamic polarities.

These three characteristics imply that the knowledge of Nature and the knowledge of oneself must go together, that a scientific fact must be perceived as a sign, that the signs correspond with one another, and that concepts borrowed from chemistry are transposable to astronomy or to human feelings. Little wonder that animal magnetism (cf. *infra*, section I, 3) is, in this philosophical current, a subject of avid interest.

The major contribution of *Naturphilosophie* to the science of the nineteenth century was the discovery of the unconscious—by the works, notably, of Gotthilf Heinrich von Schubert (*Die Symbolik des Traums*, 1814). In this very romanticism, in fact, psychoanalysis has deep roots, which began to develop with Eduard von Hartmann (*Philosophie des Unbewussten*, 1869). In this context, too, modern homeopathy came to birth with Samuel Hahnemann. Furthermore, it is not surprising that Christian theosophy, because of its own characteristics (chapter 2, section II, 2), could have inspired many *Naturphilosophen*.

Moreover, the foundation myth underpinning a number of their discourses is that of the "Redeemed Redeemer"—in other words, the theosophico-romantic narrative of a captured Light, captive but capable of being awakened ("redeemed") by another Light that had remained free. Hence the frequent use of the two terms "light" and "gravity" (*Licht* and *Schwere*) in such discourses—"gravity" rather than "darkness—the latter understood as something by which the primitive energies had originally been engulfed, but from which they tend to re-emerge. Here, the relationship with alchemy is obvious. As the historian of philosophy Jean-Louis Vieillard-Baron recently mentioned, *Naturphilosophie* is "the redemption of Nature through the thought of humankind, who alone reintegrates her into the absolute."

2. Main Representatives of This Current

The Catholic Franz von Baader (1765–1841), physician, mining engineer, and professor of philosophy at the University of Munich, greatly contributed to the emergence of *Naturphilosophie* in the Germanic countries. Let us mention in this regard especially his two essays, *Beiträge zur Elementarphysiologie* (1797) and *Ueber das pythagoräische Quadrat in der Natur* (1798). At the same time, Friedrich W. J. Schelling (1775–1854) and Carl August von Eschenmayer (1758–1862; section I, 3) also added to this impetus, the first with *Von der Weltseele* (1798), and the second with *Sätze aus der Naturmetaphysik* (1797).

In the history of philosophy, Baader occupies a position rich in fertile tensions between Schelling and Georg W. F. Hegel (1770–1831), as distant from the "naturalism" of the former as from the "idealism" of the latter. Above all, he is the most important Christian theosopher of the nineteenth century. This *Böhmius redivivus*, as he has been called, takes his place among the great hermeneuts of the thought of Boehme and of Saint-Martin, while simultaneously marking Christian theosophy with his own thought. He picks up the principal themes dear to the two latter (such as the Sophia, the ontological androgeneity of humanity, celestial objects, the successive falls, love, etc.) and reinterprets them in an original fashion while integrating the science of his time with them—notably speculations about animal magnetism. Although lacking the prophetic voice so characteristic of the theosophers of the baroque period (and still echoing in Saint-Martin), Baader's philosophical language is nonetheless strewn with dazzling insights (cf. e.g., one of his most inspired works: the *Fermenta cognitionis*, 1822–1825; French translation published in 1985). Additionally, Baader was with Julie de Krüdener one of the direct inspirers of the original project of the Holy Alliance, in the period when Tsar Alexander I was leaning toward certain forms of mysticism, and his voice long made itself heard in the liberal Catholic milieux of Europe.

Let us mention (in alphabetical order) some of the other *Naturphilosophen* whose thought is more or less characterized by theosophy or, at least, by an orientation of a pansophic type: Joseph Ennemoser (1787–1854; *Der Magnetismus in Verhältnis zur Natur und Religion*, 1842); Joseph von Görres (1776–1848; *Aphorismen*, 1802; section I, 4; section II, 1); Justinus Kerner (1786–1852; *Eine Erscheinung aus dem Nachtgebiete der Natur*, 1836); Johann Friedrich von Meyer (1772–1849; cf. especially his articles published in *Blätter für höhere Wahrheit*, 1818–1832); Novalis (pseudonym of Friedrich von Hardenberg, 1772–1801; *Das Allgemeine Brouillon* 1798–1799); Hans Christian Oersted (1777–1851; *Der Geist der Natur*, 1850–1851); Gotthilf Heinrich von Schubert (1780–1860; *Ansichten uüber die Nachtseite der Naturwissenschaft*, 1808); Johann Wilhelm Ritter (1776–1810; *Fragmente aus dem Nachlass eines jungen Physikers*, 1810); Henrik Steffens (1773–1845; *Grundzüge der philosophischen Naturwissenschaften*, 1806); Ignaz Troxler (1780–1866; *Uber das Leben und sein Problem*, 1806); and Johann Jakob Wagner (1766–1834; *Organon der menschlichen Erkenntnis*, 1830).

Gustav Theodor Fechner (1801–1887; *Zend Avesta*, 1851; section I, 4) and Carl Gustav Carus (1789–1869; *Psyche*, 1848; *Natur und Idee*, 1862) are situated in the extension of this movement that was already on the wane. Let us note that Johann Wolfgang von Goethe (1749–1832) has no real connection with it, with the possible exception of some of his scientific works, like *Uber die Spiraltendenz* (1831), and his essays on the metamorphosis of plants and on colors (*Zur Farbenlehre*, 1810).

Notwithstanding, this movement is not limited to the Germanic world. Part of the work of Saint-Martin (chapter 3, section I, 2) can be related to it; especially, his work *De l'Esprit des choses*, 1802); and for the English domain we could cite William Paley (1743–1805; *Natural Theology*, 1892), as well as Sir Humphrey Davy (1778–1829; *Consolations in Travel*, 1830).

3. *Naturphilosophie* and Animal Magnetism

One of the many publications by Justinus Kerner about animal magnetism is his famous work *Die Seherin von Prevorst* (1829, translated as *The Seeress of Prevorst*, 1855). This is an account of the visions of a young woman, Friederike Hauffe, whom he had magnetized over the course of several months. During her trances, she had held conversations about the worlds of the beyond, to which this state gave her access. Carl August von Eschenmayer, co-founder of the journal *Archiv für den thierischen Magnetismus* (1817–1826; section I, 2), commented on the visions of this woman and of others similarly magnetized. He is the author, among several works and essays relevant to this area, of *Mysterien des inneren Lebens* (1830), one of the most interesting publications of the period on the faculties of clairvoyance induced by animal magnetism.

Eschenmayer, Kerner, and many others (including Baader) held that magnetic ecstasy enables the subject to recover for a few moments the state that was ours before the original fall. They also believed that they could rediscover in the descriptions of journeys made through the celestial spheres (the "imaginal world," to employ the expression dear to Henry Corbin [chapter 5; section I, 2]) many elements of a nature to confirm the authenticity of the visions. Seventeenth-century theosophers such as Boehme, Gichtel, Lead, or Pordage (chapter 2, section II, 2), for example, had been graced with similar visions without resorting to animal magnetism (which had not yet been discovered, anyhow).

In France, Marie-Thérèse Mathieu, magnetized by G. P. Billot in the 1820s, entered into contact with her guardian angel. In his book *Arcanes de la vie future dévoilée* (1848–1860, three volumes [*The Celestial Telegraph. Or, Secrets of the Life to Come*, 1851]), the magnetizer Louis-Alphonse Cahagnet (1805–1885) relates the descriptions that his subjects Bruno Binet and Adèle Maginot gave of the celestial spaces through which they traveled. The most famous case in the

United States is that of Andrew Jackson Davis (1826–1810), who, magnetized for the first time in 1843 (in New York state), was immediately gratified with visions and revelations obtained in the course of his rambles in other worlds, and of which he later gave a detailed narrative in *The Magic Staff* (1857). This book, along with his first work, *The Principles of Nature: Her Divine Revelations* (1847), greatly contributed to his fame.

Animal magnetism was obviously not reserved for the *Naturphilosophen* alone, but was a set of practices and discourses widely disseminated in the Western world during this period. It thus entered into the common stock of ideas from which many took their religious bearings on life.

4. Esotericism on the Edge of *Naturphilosophie* (1815–1857)

In the Germany of this period appeared translations of books by Saint-Martin (G. H. von Schubert [*supra*, 3] is the author of one of them). The theosopher from Frankfurt Johann Friedrich von Meyer (*supra*, 3), of subtle and varied works, the first translator into German of the *Sepher Yetzirah* (chapter 1, section III, 1) and especially the author of a new German translation of the Bible, touched on almost all the sciences known as "occult." His review *Blätter für höhere Wahrheit* ("Pages for a Higher Truth," 1818–1832; *supra*, section III, 1), of which he was the main contributor, constitutes in this aspect one of the most interesting documents of the period. Again in Germany, three works appeared that sketched a history of "magic": *Geschichte der Magie* (1822), by Joseph Ennemoser, *Zauberbibliothek* (1821–1826) by Georg Konrad Horst, and the last part of *Christliche Mystik* (1836–1842) by Joseph Görres (section I, 2; section II, 1).

In France, Antoine Fabre d'Olivet (chapter 3, section I, 3) pursued his pagan-oriented work; his *Histoire philosophique du genre humain* (1822–1824), a vast fresco with an ambitious purpose, would be highly prized by the "occultists" of the end of the century. The book of Ferdinand Davis, *Tableau des sciences occultes* (1830), and the first writings of Cahagnet (section I, 3), are already a prefiguration of what would become the occultist current with Éliphas Lévi (section II, 2). After *Philosophie de l'infini* (1814) and *Messianisme* (1831–1839) of the Pole

Hoëné-Wronski (section II, 2), there was no dearth of researchers of universal keys, such as Giovanni Malfatti di Montereggio's *Studien über Anarchie und Hierarchie des Wissens* 1845). Simultaneously conservative and close to socalist utopias, Pierre-Simon Ballanche, influenced by the Illuminist current, occupies a respectable place in the landscape of the political philosophy of his period (*Essais de palingénésie sociale*, 1827; *La Vision d'Hébal*, 1831). The abbot Paul François Gaspard Lacuria, author of *Harmonies de l'Être exprimées par les nombres* (1847), found in theosophy the key to music and arithmology. Hortensius Flamel (who is perhaps Éliphas Lévi), author of a *Livre d'or* and a *Livre rouge* (1842), attempted to combine Fourierism and Hermetism.

One of the representatives of swedenborgian theosophy was Jean-Jacques Bernard who, in his work *Opuscules théosophiques* (1822), attempted to reconcile the theosophies of Saint-Martin and of Swedenborg. Edouard Richer and, especially, Jacques F. E. Le Boys des Guays actively propagated the teachings of the same Swedenborg. A messianism introduced in France by the Poles Adam Mickiewcz and André Towianki in the 1840s would greatly influence Éliphas Lévi (section II, 2), just as Hoëné-Wronski would do directly (cf. *supra*). Let us note finally that, in the course of this period extending to 1847, alchemical production seems moribund despite—at least, for France—a *Hermès dévoilé* (1832) by Cyliani (a little book that was to enjoy a lasting success), and a *Cours de philosophie hermétique* (1843) signed by Cambriel.

Ambiguous relationships were cultivated between the esoteric currents and the most picturesque of the socialist utopias, perceptible in Alphonse Esquiros (*De la Vie future du point de vue socialiste*, 1850) or in Jean Reynaud's Druidism (*Terre et Ciel*, 1854). These relationships clearly intertwined in Charles Fourier, the "Ariosto of the utopians," not so much by the content as by the style of the discourse (see his *Théorie des quatre mouvements*, 1807) His descriptions occasionally bear some resemblance to certain visionary narratives of Swedenborg, of which they sometimes seem an involuntary parody.

After 1848, even more than hitherto, Swedenborgianism was tinged by humanitarian prophesy, as in the illuminated socialism of a Louis Lucas (*Une Révolution dans la musique*, 1849), of a Jean-Marie Ragon de Bettignies (*Orthodoxie maçonnique* and *Maçonnerie occulte*,

1853) or of a Henri Delaage (*Le Monde occulte*, 1851). Also marking these years, two substantial essays on alchemy would remain great classics in the eyes of many adepts of this "traditional science": *A Suggestive Enquiry into the Hermetic Mystery* (1850), by Mary Ann Atwood; and *Alchemy and the Alchemists* (1857), by Ethan Allen Hitchcock. These years were marked, finally, by the fine book of Frédéric Portal, *Les Couleurs symboliques* (1857), the *Zend-Avesta* (1851) of Gustav Theodor Fechner (section I, 2) and the first great anthology of texts of Christian theosophy (*Stimmen aus dem Heiligthum der christlichen Theosophie*, 1851), collected and edited by Julius Hamberger, a close disciple of Baader.

5. Esotericism in Art (1815–1847)

In the seventeenth century, a natural symbiosis occurred between the baroque *imaginaire* and theosophical literature. The same was true of the latter and romanticism, although this relationship is more evident in Germanic countries than elsewhere. If we grant that the synthetic spirit (the taste for global approaches) and the suffering related to the limited human condition comprise the two major characteristics of European romanticism (and of many forms of *gnosis*), then we better understand that the theosophical discourses related to the myth of the fall and the reintegration could find a hearing among many romantics. Some historians (like Léon Cellier) could even claim, and rightly so, that this myth largely subtends most literary and philosophical productions of that movement.

In France, a certain number of authors, and not the least of them, continued to respond to public taste for these great themes that Illuminism had developed. Thus, regarding novels, Honoré de Balzac was open to inspiration from Saint-Martin and Swedenborg (*Louis Lambert*, 1832; *Séraphita* and *Le Livre mystique*, 1835). A similar inspiration runs through *Consuelo* (1845) by George Sand. The purpose is more didactic and explicit in *Le Magicien* (1836) by Alphonse Esquiros, or in England *Zanoni* (1842) by Sir Edward G. Bulwer-Lytton (section II, 2). This Rosicrucian novel has continued, until today, to inspire many dreams and exegeses of all sorts.

This period also saw Goethe, shortly before his demise in 1832, give his *Faust* the final touches. Theosophy tinges, sometimes deeply, the *Carnets* (*Notebooks*) of Joseph Joubert, kept assiduously from 1786 to his death in 1824. The posthumous writings of the painter Philipp Otto Runge (chapter 3, section III, 3), published in 1840–1841, are saturated with thoughts of a theosophical type bearing on art. Of course, magnetism is the subject of many literary adaptations, like *Der Magnetiseur* (1817), by Ernst T. A. Hoffmann, *Mesmeric Revelation* (1844) and *The Facts in the Case of Mr. Valdemar* (1845), by Edgar Allen Poe—all works heralding a genre of writing (the classic "fantastic" literature") that would flourish starting in the middle of the century.

II. Universal Tradition and Occultism

I. From the Romantic East to the India of the Theosophical Society

At the end of the eighteenth century, images of India had begun deeply to penetrate the Western *imaginaire*. However, the East was especially a discovery of romanticism; compare, for example, the writings of Joseph Görres (section I, 2, 4) on Asian myths (*Mythengeschichte des asiatischen Welt*, 1810) and of Friedrich Schlegel on India (*Ueber die Sprache und Weisheit der Inder*, 1808). These publications, like the general interest in the fairy tales (*Kinder- und Hausmärchen*, 1812–1815, published by Jacob and Wilhelm Grimm), myths, and legends of Europe, belong to the romantic quest for the One. This quest would contribute to revive the idea of *philosophia perennis*, progressively spread to all the traditions of the world, no longer limited to those of the Mediterranean universe, as was still the case in the Renaissance (chapter 2, section I, 1).

The word "Tradition" appears in the German title of a book that would stand out in history, that of Franz Joseph Molitor on Kabbalah (*Philosophie der Geschichte oder über die Tradition*, 1827), followed by *La Kabbale* of Adolphe Franck (1843). In another scholarly work (Jacques Matter, *Histoire du gnosticisme*, 1828) appears the first use found hitherto of the substantive "esotericism" (cf. *supra*, beginning of the introduction). To this, we may add two obsessive themes: that of the mysteries of the Great Pyramid (John Taylor, *The Great Pyramid*, 1858) and that of Druidism interpreted as the mother religion of humanity. The speculations on the Great Pyramid understandably went together with something like a return of the Hermetist current. For example, in the collection *Das Kloster*, which he directed in Stuttgart from 1849 to 1860, Johann Scheible put into circulation, alongside works by Agrippa and many treatises on magic, a German translation of the *Corpus Hermeticum* (*CH*; according to the 1706 edition; chapter 3, section I, 1). In 1866, Louis Ménard published *Hermès Trismégiste* (his translation of major texts of the *CH*, preceded by an introduction). The book would stimulate new translations and glosses (section II, 3), mostly works by personalities connected with the Theosophical Society or with neo-Rosicrucian Orders.

Founded in 1875, the Theosophical Society (TS) favored the success of this idea of a "universal Tradition" that, at the beginning of the twentieth century, would be labeled "primordial"—the better to define it as the mother of all the others (chapter 5, section II, 1). Helena Petrovna Blavatsky (1831–1991; section III, 2), the principal founder (chapter 4, section II, 2) of the TS, contributed much to it herself through her own works, destined for a lasting success (*Isis Unveiled*, 1877; *The Secret Doctrine*, 1888). Edouard Schuré defended the existence of a Primordial Tradition in his book *Les Grands Initiés* (1889), a bestseller often translated and republished. In it we find again (as in the Renaissance, chapter 2, section1, 1) a list—a chain—of ancient "Sages" of the *philosophia perennis*, but now flanked with other more exotic names (his list is composed of Rama, Krishna, Hermes, Moses, Orpheus, Pythagoras, Plato, and Jesus). At the end of the century, the emergence of a science of comparative religions and the assembly of a great Parliament of Religions in Chicago (1893) contributed to the dissemination of the expression "Primordial Tradition."

2. Advent of Spiritualism and Occultism (1847–1860)

During the first half of the century, animal magnetism had met (section I, 3) with wonderful success, one of the original forms that it had taken being narratives, by "magnetized" subjects, bearing on questions about the supernatural world. Now, in 1848, in the United States (one year after the publication of the book by Andrew Jackson Davis quoted *supra*, section I, 3), the spiritualist movement emerged. The sisters Margaretta and Catherine Fox, in Hydesville, New York, heard a mysterious repeated knocking in the house on the night of March 31, 1848. Thinking it might be a message of some sort, they worked out a code that might enable them to respond and ask questions of their own. The belief that the knocking entity was the spirit of a deceased person soon followed. Thus, a new practice of communication with spirits had come to birth, called Spiritualism, which quickly spread through the United States and then through the rest of the Western world. As we have seen, in the preceding decades, the subjects of animal magnetism entered into relationship with entities—not only with non-human, but also with deceased people. However, in Spiritualism it is essentially with the latter that spiritualists would henceforth try to establish rapport.

Spiritualism does not pertain directly to the history of esoteric currents properly speaking, but it has connections with them by the influence that it exerted everywhere and by the problems that it posed to esotericists of all kinds. Its blossoming and the quasi-simultaneous appearance of the literary genre known as the "fantastic," in its classical form (section I, 5), coincide with the triumph of the industrial revolution (Karl Marx's *Manifesto* dates from 1847), which is not by happenstance. One of the first outstanding theoricians of Spiritualism in the United States was Andrew Jackson Davis (cf. *supra*), who first looked askance at this new trend but eventually became won over to it. In France Denizard Hyppolyte Léon Rivail (*alias* Allen Kardec, 1804–1869, *Le Monde des esprits*, 1857) aimed to make Spiritualism into a "religion" tinged with sentimentalism and rationalism. Kardec elevated to the rank of an actual dogma the idea of reincarnation. Less frequently adopted by the English-speaking spiritualists of that time, this idea harmonized well with the egalitarian, socialist, and utopian tendencies of the era (section I, 4).

It was also in the mid-nineteenth century that Occultism (in the sense of "the occultist current") emerged. One of its first outstanding representatives was a man whose youth had been dedicated to utopian and humanitarian ideas (he was even sentenced as a revolutionary)—

namely, Alphonse-Louis Constant (*alias* Éliphas Lévi, 1810–1875). He may have been influenced by Hoëné Wronski (section I, 4), whom he met in 1852. Keenly interested in practical magic and theurgy, he would have evoked the spirit of Apollonius of Tyana in 1854. An unmethodical compiler but a gifted synthesizer, this magus inspired conviction and his appearance was timely. His works *Dogme et ritual de la Haute magie* (1854–1856), *Histoire de la magie* (1860), and *La Clef des Grands Mystères* (1861)—to cite only a few of them—would mark the whole occultist current. The year 1860, moreover, saw the publication, at the same time as his *Histoire de la magie*, of two other works (not "esoterically" committed): *Histoire du merveilleux* by Louis Figuier, and *La Magie et l'astrologie* by Alfred Maury.

3. Growth of Occultism in the Era of Scienticism and Continuity of Theosophy (1860–1914)

The rise of scienticism (the claim that science is the only means of knowledge and that there is no other reality than that based on ordinary perception) was eroding faith in spiritual matters. Facing it was the occultist current (Occultism), an extension of what had begun to be known shortly before as the "occult sciences" (cf. Ferdinand Denis, section I, 4). This current appeared as an alternative solution—or, rather, as a new response *from* modernity confronted *with* itself, more than as a response *to* modernity proper (cf. introduction, section II, last paragraph). In fact, the occultists were not opposed to modernity and did not consider scientific progress as noxious; they sought instead to integrate them into a global vision capable of bringing out the vacuity of materialism. We recognize here something resembling an echo of the program of the *Naturphilosophen*. However, the occultists are distinguished from them by a more marked taste for "pragmatic evidence" ("scientific proofs") related to the reality of certain "phenomena" appearing to prove the existence of several orders of reality, and often for various forms of practical "magic"—in a world that seemed definitively disenchanted. Occultism is linked by affinity to the symbolist current in literature and in the arts (section III, 1), just as *Naturphilosophie* was to romanticism.

After Éliphas Lévi (section II, 2), a few strong personalities dominate a rather disparate crowd. In France, Gérard Encausse (*alias* Papus; 1865–1915; section III, 1), a physician, nicknamed "the Balzac of Occultism" (his work is prolific), is considered still today by a great many admirers as a magus, a true "initiate." His *Traité de science occulte* appeared in 1888, as did the first number of his periodical *L'Initiation*. The Society for Psychical Research was founded in London in 1882 and several important initiatic associations would see the light of day (*infra*, section II). In company with his friend Anthelme-Nizier Philippe (known as "Maître Philippe of Lyons"), Papus went to Saint Petersburg to visit Nicholas II and the Tsarina on two occasions; he introduced them, they claim, to Martinism.

One of those that Papus called his spiritual masters was Joseph Alexandre Saint-Yves d'Alveydre, inventor toward 1900 of a "magical Archeometer" (a key revealing the correspondences among many domains of knowledge) and author of penetrating studies on musical esotericism. Also close to Papus by his purpose and by his work was Stanislas de Guaita (1861–1897; *Essais de Sciences maudites*; 1886; *Le Temple de Satan*, 1891; section II, I), one of the most famous authors of this current. Let us cite again Josephin Péladan (section III, 1, 3) in whom Occultism takes an artistic and literary form, as well as Charles Henry (1859–1926) and especially Albert Faucheux (*alias* François-Charles Barlet; *L'Occultisme*, 1909)—one of the principal figures, in France, of this same current. Paul Vulliaud was not an occultist, but the journal *Les Entretiens idéalistes* that he founded in 1906, and the artistic and literary movement that he motivated, are nevertheless part of this landscape.

Among the Russians appears in first place Piotr Dem'ianovich Ouspensky (chapter 5, section II, 3), the author, notably, of *Tertium Organum* (Russian edition in 1912, English in 1920), which presents an interesting philosophy of Nature, considerations on the Tarot, dreams, etc. In Prague, several esoterically oriented centers were active around 1900. In the Netherlands, Occultism is represented notably by Fredéric Van Eeden (*Het Hypnotisme en de Wonderen*, 1887), in Germany by Carl du Prel (*Studien aus dem Gebiete der Geheimwissenschaften*, 1894–1895) and especially Franz Hartmann (1838–1912;

Magic White and Black, 1886; *Cosmology or Universal Science*, 1888; section III, 1, 2, 3). A discussion of certain representatives of this occultist current in England, including Aleister Crowley, follows *infra* and section III. Let us add finally that astrology experienced a new vogue in the years between 1880 and 1914; it occupied a prominent place in occultist literature and several specialized works (e.g., those of William Frederick Allan, *alias* Alan Leo, 1860–1917) attempt to confer greater credibility on it.

After the publications already mentioned (section II, 1), which come within the extension of neo-Alexandrian Hermetism, let us cite a few of those of the occultist period properly speaking, also matched with very "hermeticizing" commentaries. They are the editions provided by the two famous "Rosicrucians" Hargrave Jennings and Pachal Beverly Randolph (section III, 1)—respectively in Madras in 1884 and in Toledo, Ohio, in 1889—and by Anna Bonus Kingsford (also author of several works, including *The Perfect Way* (1881; section III, 1, 2) and Edward Maitland, under the title *The Virgin of the World*, 1885. The most erudite of all, due to George Robert Stowe Mead (*Corpus Hermeticum*, 1906), would long be authoritative, even in academia.

In fact, unlike many commentators of the *CH* in his period, Mead is the author not only of many publications belonging to occultist thought (thus, *Quests New and Old*, 1913), but also of scholarly works pertaining to esoteric currents. It is the same for the works of another Englishman, Sir Arthur Edward Waite (1857–1942; section III, 1), a very important author whose works are resolutely in the line of the occultist movement of his period but that are not without scholarly merits (he wrote many works on the history of Freemasonry, Rosicrucianism, alchemy, Christian theosophy, etc.). William Wynn Westcott (section III, 1), another notable figure of this milieu in England, also strove—but with much less effectiveness and scope than Waite—to make known the riches of the Western esoteric currents of the past (thus, through his series *Collectanea Hermetica*, 1993–1902).

Between theosophers and occultists, the frontier is sometimes fluid, either because some of the latter (such as François-Charles

Barlet; section II, 3) were also, in a certain manner, theosophers, or because they published earlier writings belonging to this current. Thus, Papus edited the letters of Martines de Pasqually and of Saint-Martin, and René Philipon, who signed as "Chevalier de la Rose Croissante," provided in 1899 the very first edition of the *Traité de la Réintégration des Êtres* by this same Pasqually (chapter 3, section I, 2). Nevertheless closer to this current was, for example, the Russian Vladimir Solovyov, Nature philosopher and sophiologist (in Russian: *Lectures on Theanthropy*, 1877–1881; *The Beauty of Nature*, 1889; *The Meaning of Love*, 1892–1894). We could not say that Rudolf Steiner (1861–1925), Nature philosopher and prolific author, is very closely connected with it.

Starting in his student years in Vienna, Steiner was concerned with natural sciences and physics, in the wake of Goethe, whose scientific works he co-edited (1883–1897). Thenceforth, he would never cease to meditate on the "esoteric" meaning of the teachings of the genius of Weimar (*Goethe als Theosoph*, 1904; his essays on Goethe's *Faust* and *Märchen* date from 1918). His production includes many essays, various treatises (*Theosophie*, 1904; Die *Geheimwissenschaft in Umriss*, 1910), innumerable lectures (most of them are published), and a few dramas (section III, 3).

In line with the Christocentric evolutionism that characterizes his thought, he insisted on the necessity of fully assuming the knowledge of the spiritual history of the West in view of its transmutation, and not relying on a Primordial Tradition from which we would passively expect manifestations in the form of new divine avatars. Therefore, the introduction, by the TS, of the young Krishnamurti as a Christ come back to earth caused Steiner to break away from this Society in 1913. Humanity on its journey must always, he held, work to find balance between two poles, the cosmic forces of expansion (opening of the being, aspiration toward the heights, but also egocentrism) and the forces of concentration (hardening, materialization). Reincarnation and "karma" play the role of instruments of liberation. To distinguish it firmly from the teachings of the TS, Steiner called his system "Anthroposophy," and gave this name to the Society that he founded in 1913 (the Anthroposophical Society).

III. Esotericism in Initiatic Societies and in Art (1848–1914)

I. Masonic or Paramasonic Societies

In Masonry, it is especially (cf. chapter 3, section I, 1) the Higher Grade Systems that draw inspiration from the esoteric currents. After the Revolution, the Rectified Scottish Rite continued in Switzerland; the Ancient and Accepted Scottish Rite remained alive, too—as well as a part of "Egyptian" Masonry, notably through the presence of the Rites of Memphis and of Mishraim. At the end of the nineteenth century, we can observe the same phenomenon as about a hundred years earlier—namely, the creation and the proliferation of new Societies of this type.

In 1868, Paschal Beverly Randolph (1825–1875; section II, 3) founded the most ancient Rosicrucian group in the United States, the Fraternitas Rosae Crucis. Thereafter, in 1876, the Swedenborgian Rite known as the Illuminated Theosophists (chapter 3, section III, 2) returned from America to Europe. Of a distinctly Christian orientation, the Societas Rosicruciana in Anglia (SRIA), branching from regular English Freemasonry, includes Higher Grades inspired by those of the Gold- und Rosenkreuzer of the eighteenth century (chapter 3, section III, 2). Born in London in 1867, it is the creation of learned occultists such as Robert Wentworth Little (1840–1918) and Kenneth R. H. Mackenzie (1833–1886). Bulwer-Lytton (section I, 1; section II, 2) and Éliphas Lévi were honorary members; William Wynn Westcott (section II, 3) was its Supremus Magus from 1891 to 1925.

The year 1888 saw the birth in France of a Rose-Croix Kabbalistique, founded by Guaïta (section II, 2) and Péladan (section III, 3), which would go through many fragmentations and estrangements. The year 1891 saw the birth of the Martinist Order, a creation of Papus (the adjective refers to the names Martines de Pasqually and Louis-Claude de Saint-Martin), which, from its incipience, has always accepted women as members. We have seen (section II, 3) that Nicolas II—open to the "occult" as were the last Romanovs—would have been a member. The year 1888 saw the emergence of the Fraternitas (a creation of Franz Hartmann (section II, 3; section III, 2, 3) in Germany, and of the Order of the Golden Dawn (GD) in England, which also accepted women (it was an outgrowth of the SRIA). Created by Westcott (cf. *supra*), William Robert Woodman and Samuel Liddell MacGregor Mathers, the GD drew inspiration from the Kabbalah as well as the Tarot; it gave an important place to ceremonial magic (which is not the case of the SRIA).

An English translation, by Samuel L. MacGregor Mathers, of *The Book of the Sacred Magic of Abra-Melin the Mage* (a theurgic ritual in Latin, from an old manuscript of uncertain prevenance and period) was published in 1898, and then circulated in the form of a Rite known to the members of the GD. The celebrated writer William Butler Yeats, who was initiated into the GD in 1888, directed it for several months. Aleister Crowley (1875–1947; chapter 5, section I, 1; section III, 1)—probably the most famous figure of the whole occultist movement in England—after joining in 1898, remained a member for only eighteen months. Waite (section II, 3) was a member starting in 1891. The Stella Matutina created in 1903 is a branch of it. Between 1906 and 1910, the occultist Theodor Reuss established the Ordo Templi Orientis (OTO), a Lodge for research in secret sciences whose destiny was also directed by Aleister Crowley. The latter further organized its rituals, endowing them with a more pronounced sexual and anti-Christian aspect. He created in parallel, in 1909, an Astrum Argentinum that is founded on the teachings of the GD. Rudolf Steiner, who probably was never a member of the OTO, created his own Anthroposophical Society in Dornach, near Basel (section II, 3), which is not of a masonic type. Another important organization is the Rosicrucian Fellowship, creation of Carl Louis von Grasshoff (*alias* Max Heindel) in 1907 and whose world center is located in Oceanside, California.

There existed other circles, associations, and movements. Thus, the Mouvement Cosmique, founded around 1900 by Max Théon—continuation of the Hermetic Brotherhood of Luxor—produced starting in 1903 an enormous body of work entitled *Tradition cosmique*, dedicated to the "original tradition." Some of these movements assembled Christians; this is the case for the Hermetic Academy of Anna Bonus Kingsford (section II, 3; section III, 2). In France, Yvon Le Loup (*alias* Paul Sédir, 1871–1926), collaborator of Papus, led the group known as *Les Amitiés Spirituelles*. The Jesuit Victor Drevon and Alexis de Sarachaga created in 1873 a center of esoteric studies at Paray-le-Monial, the Hieron. This list is partial; it does not include many groupings and associations that exceed the limits of our purpose, as for example the Gnostic Church founded in 1890 by Jules Doinel.

2. The Theosophical Society

Founded in 1875 in New York by Helena Petrovna Blavatsky ("H. P.B.," 1831–1891; section II, 1), Henry Steel Olcott and William Quan Judge, the TS—which is not masonic in character—went through various forms and ramifications in the course of its history but that have preserved the same common denominators. "Theosophism," a generic term used to describe its orientation, does not set forth a "doctrine" properly speaking, although the title of the book of H.P.B., *The Secret Doctrine* (1888; preceded by *Isis Unveiled*, 1877) customarily serves as a reference for the theosophists (in English, this term distinguishes them from the theosophers of the "classical" Christian theosophical current).

At its foundation in 1875, the TS fixed a triple goal for itself, respected by the branches issued from it. These were, first, to form the nucleus of a universal fellowship; second, to encourage the study of all the religions, of philosophy, and of science; and third, to study the laws of Nature as well as the psychical and spiritual powers of the human being. By its content and its inspiration, it is largely dependent on Eastern spiritualities, especially Hindu; in this, it well reflects the cultural climate in which it was born. H.P.B. and her Society never tired of affirming the unity of all the religions in their "esoteric" foundations, and of trying to develop, among those people who had the desire for it, the faculty of becoming "true theosophists." In its beginnings especially, the TS devoted a good share of its activities to the "psychical" or "metaphysical," areas that were objects of vivid interest at the time. Departed for India in 1878, H.P.B. founded there in 1879 her journal *The Theosophist* and established, there too, in 1883 (at Adyar, near Madras, India) the official seat of her Society. The latter was well accepted by the natives of the country, more especially in view of the climate of tolerance that reigned within this movement. H.P.B. returned to Europe in 1885.

The history of the branches of the TS after the death of its founder in 1891 is rich and complex; let us mention notably the creation in 1909, by Robert Crosbie, of the United Lodge of Theosophists. Three factors favored the influence of this movement, implanted in most Western countries.

The first is the presence of significant personalities, such as Annie Besant (1847–1933), its president starting in 1907, Franz Hartmann (founder of a German branch in 1886; section II, 3; III, 1, 2), and Rudolf Steiner (general secretary of the German section in 1902). Steiner broke away from the TS in 1913 (chapter 4, section III, 2), of which the inclination for Eastern traditions seemed to him irreconcilable with the Christian and Western character of his own orientation. Before him and for this same reason, Anna Bonus Kingsford, an influential figure of a feminine and Christian Occultism in the years 1870 and 1880 (section II, 3; section III, 1), broke away from it to establish a Hermetic Society penetrated by Christianity. However, in creating their own organizations, personalities like Steiner, and to a lesser degree Anna Kingsford, contributed to spread, even in a modified form, teachings issued from their mother Society.

The second factor comprises the many links that the various branches have maintained with most of the other Societies of this type. Thus, the international Spiritist and Spiritualist Congress of 1889 and the Masonic and Spiritualist Congress of 1908, which met in Paris, represent a good example of this crossroads of ideas and of tendencies. Moreover, the frontiers differentiating most of these movements from one another were rather permeable; it is instead inside each one of them that oppositions were enacted, that people fulminated "excommunications."

The third factor, finally, is obviously the great number of artists having manifestly undergone the influence of the TS—a point that is the subject of part of the following section.

3. Esoteric Arts and Literature

Among the great French writers that drew from the referential corpus of the esoteric currents appears Gérard de Nerval (*Voyage en Orient*, 1851; *Les Illuminés*, 1852; *Les Chimères*, 1854). The sonnet by Charles

Baudelaire ("Correspondances," around 1857) has become a sort of poetic *Emerald Tablet*, and the texts of this author on the notion of creative imagination are not without affinities with what is one of the components of the esoteric "form of thought" (cf. introduction, section IV). The thematic range in *Contemplations* (1856) of Victor Hugo is close to that of the most classical Christian theosophy (let us also recall that between 1853 and 1855, in Jersey and in Guernsey, Hugo the spiritualist conversed with Dante and Shakespeare). In Villiers de L'Isle-Adam, Occultism found one of its best authors of fiction (*Isis*, 1862; *Axël*, 1888); it is also present in Saint-Pol-Roux (*Les Reposoirs de la Procession*, 1893), and for Josephin Péladan (section II, 3; section III, 1) it inspired an impressive saga (*L'Éthopée*, 1886–1907). In Paris, the exhibitions of the Salons de la Rose-Croix, connected with the Order founded by Péladan (section II, 3), are one of the most aesthetically fertile episodes in the occultist current; from 1893 to 1898, one could admire there the works of Félicien Rops; Georges Rouault and Erik Satie took part in it. In the same period, a few works of "Rosicrucian" fiction also appeared in the wake of Bulwer-Lytton's *Zanoni* (section I, 5). Examples are the novel by Franz Hartmann, *An Adventure among the Rosicrucians* (1887; section II, 3; section III, 1, 2) and one by Emma Hardinge Britten, *Ghostland, or Researches into the Mysteries of Occultism* (1876)—one of the principal works of fiction inspired by the occultist current and animal magnetism.

The musical production work of Richard Wagner, from 1843 to 1882, incarnated for the Belle Époque the idea of music elevated to the rank of religion. Both his texts and scores remain a privileged place of hermeneutics. However, the existence of any "esotericism" in his work is mostly in the minds of certain readers and listeners. This remark would also apply to the reception of the work of painters such as Arnold Böcklin or Gustave Moreau. Like Wagner in Bayreuth, Rudolf Steiner created at Dornach (near Basel), the seat of his Anthroposophical Society, a *Gesamtkunstwerk* (a "total artistic work" like Wagner's project, of a very Germanic nature). It was the "Goethanum" (chapter 5, section III, 1), a building meant to reflect the very spirit of the Society and to be a site appropriate for the performance of dramas (principally of those that he authored: *Die Pforte der Einweihung*, 1910; *Die Prüfung der Seele*, 1911; *Der Hüter der Schwelle*, 1912; *Der Seelen Erwachen*, 1913).

5

Esotericisms of the Twentieth Century

I. Gnoses in the Wake of the Western "Tradition"

I. "Traditional Sciences," Christian Theosophy, and New Forms of *Gnosis*

Surviving in the form of activities as much speculative as opera-tive, practiced inside initiatic associations or by individuals, the so-called "traditional" sciences (i.e., especially astrology, alchemy, and "magic") directly touched a broad public. The most popular is evi-dently astrology, "queen" of the divinatory Arts. What big bookstore does not dedicate entire bookshelves to it, taking over most of the "esoteric" or "occult" section? What media does not have its column of daily or weekly advice? In its most widespread aspect—simplistic predictions, flat utilitarianism—it answers the more or less conscious need to rediscover in our world, which many consider too uncentered and fragmented, the *Unus mundus*, the unity of the universe and of humanity, through a language founded on the principle of univer-sal correspondences. When this need leads to a concept of astrology that does not reduce it to a mere "mancy" (just an instrument of divination), but that induces the practice of a form of hermeneutics of "signs," then we can see in it a form of *gnosis* that connects it with esoteric currents properly speaking. After Alan Leo (chapter 4, section II, 3), many in the twentieth century, from Karl Brandler-Pracht (1864–1945) to André Barbault, including Daniel Chennev-ière (alias Dane Rudhyar, 1895–1985), have considered it as such and contributed, more or less successfully, to confer on it a status in its own right in the humanities.

Since Alliette (chapters 1–3), the Tarot has become another esoteric current in its own right, composed of an ever-increasing referential corpus. The Tarot serves not only to tell fortunes, but also to practice a form of *gnosis* drawing from other traditions, like Kabbalah—thus, with Aleister Crowley (*The Book of Thoth*, 1944; section III, 1; chapter 4, section III, 1). Among other exegetes of the Tarot, let us cite Marc Haven (*Le Tarot*, 1937), Gérard Van Rijnberk (*Le Tarot*, 1946), Paul Marteau (*Le Tarot de Marseille*, 1949), and Valentin Tomberg (*Meditationen*, 1972; *infra*, 2).

As in the past, the alchemical domain is divided between the "blowers" (*souffleurs*, a French epithet for alchemists whose goal is almost solely for material gain) and the "Philosophers" (those who pursue a spiritual goal, in addition to being "operative"). Some of these occasionally have organizations, like the Paracelsus Research Society, in Salt Lake City, Utah, and then in Australia, directed by Albert Richard Riedel (*alias* Frater Albertus, 1911–1984). Likewise, the Soluna laboratories, in Bavaria, were created by a notable neo-Paracelsian alchemist, Alexander von Bernus (1880–1965), who also was the author of a relatively abundant work in the tradition of German Romanticism. Outside of such associations, alchemical practice rather preserved the character of a private religion that it always has the tendency to assume.

Rare are the "Philosophers" of the twentieth century having left interesting written work. This explains in part the success of those who produced one, such as Eugène Léon Canseliet (1899–1982), whose reputation also owes much to the mystery surrounding his master Fulcanelli. This master, whose biography remains unknown, has left a *Mystère des cathédrales* (1926; *The Mystery of the Cathedrals*) as well as *Les Demeures philosophales* (1930; *The Dwellings of the Philosophers*, 1999). His disciple Canseliet has authored a few various works, among which were *Deux logis alchimiques* (1945) and *Alchimie* (1964). Both were as concerned with detecting the "alchemical signatures" on the stones of certain buildings as with seeking the Philosopher's Stone.

Other authors involved with this "science" dealt with its spiritual or initiatic aspects without necessarily being working practitioners (thus Julius Evola, *La Tradizione ermetica*, 1931; section II, 1). Alchemy has continued to occupy a good place in contemporary Western culture. Reprints and facsimile reproductions (texts and images) became easily available especially in the 1970s and 1980s. Furthermore, many historians have written about it (section III, 2). "Magic" belongs to the esoteric currents of the twentieth century insofar as it is viewed as not just a practice to procure material gratifications. On this understanding, we find it spread especially within societies and various groupings. The historian Massimo Introvigne (section III, 3) has put forward a distinction, debatable but convenient, between two categories: ceremonial magic and initiatic magic. The first would emphasize knowledge and/or powers, the effectiveness of rites. The second would stress the legitimacy of initiatic filiation, the condition of an "authentic" transformation of the member elect. Both "magics" were practiced in the hothouses of secret societies, of which several produced a rather abundant literature (this was the case of several of the works cited in this chapter 5). As for the first category, one of its most famous representatives was Aleister Crowley, already mentioned regarding the occultist current (section III, 2; chapter 4, section III, 1) and whose work and "initiatic" activities were manifold (*The Equinox of the Gods*, 1936) until the 1940s (section III, 1).

If the current of Christian Kabbalah had since long run dry, Jewish Kabbalah and, notably, the Sephirotic tree continued nonetheless to inspire many researchers in quest of a key to *gnosis*, but often by cutting them from the original Hebraic cultural terrain; (Ramon Llull and Giordano Bruno had already done the same). It is tempting, indeed, to use this tree as a support of meditation, a tool of thought. Taking this approach was Raymond Abellio (1907–1986; section III, 1; *La Bible, document chiffré*, 1950; *La Fin de l'ésotérisme*, 1973). In fact, for minds not rooted in the Jewish tradition, the corpus of Greek and Latin references lends itself more easily to a hermeneutic of a spiritual order. For that matter, the neo-Alexandrian current (chapter 4, section III, 1, 3) did not run dry in the twentieth century, as persistent interest in the *Corpus Hermeticum* bears testimony, notably several new editions completed by exegetic commentaries (of a neo-Rosicrucian character, in particular). Among these are the publications of the Shrine of Wisdom in 1923, the book by Duncan Greenless (*The Gospel of Hermes*, 1949), and that by Jan van Rijckenborgh (*De Egyptische oergnosis*, 1960–1965; section II, 2).

2. Presence of Christian Theosophy

The main representatives of a properly Christian theosophy were mostly German, Russian, and French. Rudolf Steiner continued his personal work (*Mein Lebensgang*, autobiography published in 1925; study on the *Chymische Hochzeit* of Andreae, 1917–1918), marked less by this current properly speaking than by certain aspects of the *Naturphilosophie* of the preceding century. The influence of Leopold Ziegler (1881–1958; *Ueberlieferung and Menschwerdung*, 1948; *Gestalt-wandel der Götter*, 1922) was more subtle. This sage residing on the shores of Lake Constance shared with René Guénon (section II, 1) the idea of a primordial Tradition that was fragmented, eclipsed, and forgotten. If he scrutinized myths and studied religions, however, it was more as a disciple of Boehme and of Baader, as a theosopher attentive to the symbolism of the phases of alchemical transmutation. Thus he placed Sophia at the very heart of his *gnosis*, associating her with a philosophy of Nature inseparable from a philosophy of History—itself conceived as a whole, as much biological as spiritual.

The Orthodox Church, which dedicated to Sophia the celebrated Cathedrals of Saint Sophia in Constantinople and Kiev, generally made this personage a real, central figure, contrary to what happened in Western Christianity, where she was never very present except in the Christian theosophical current. However, Sophia being one theme among others in the repertory of great images, the fact of integrating her into a theology does not necessarily imply that one is "theosophizing." This remark obtains regarding Father Paul Florensky (*La Colonne et le fondement de la vérité*, 1914 [*The Pillar and Ground of the Truth*, 2004]), and Father Sergei Bulgakov (*La Sagesse de Dieu*, 1936 [*Sophia: the Wisdom of God*, 1993], *Du verbe incarné*, 1943; *Le Paraclet*, 1946). Inspired not only by Vladimir Solovyov but also by Florensky, Tommaso Palamidessi founded an initiatic Order in Turin in 1948, Loto + Croce, which became the Associazione Archeosofica in 1968. Closer to Germanic theosophy than Florensky or Bulgakov, we find Nicholas Berdiaev (1874–1948; *Le Sens de la création*, 1916

[*The Meaning of the Creative Act*, 1955 [1916 in Russian]; *Études sur Jacob Boehme*, 1930; *Spirit and Reality*, 1957 [1946 in Russian]), a Russian philosopher established in France. Berdiaev, a great admirer of Boehme (whom he considered "a summit of the visionary power of humanity") and of Baader, proved critical with regard to what he called "occultism." On the latter, he wrote, in *The Meaning of the Creative Act*, "the great meaning" is nevertheless "to be already turned toward the cosmic secret and toward humanity's part in it." In the same movement, he sharply criticized the teachings of the Theosophical Society and those of Rudolf Steiner because of the evolutionism that is part of their system, and saw in them "a serious symptom of the decomposition of the physical plane of Being" (*The Meaning of Creation*).

If Christian theosophy was but one aspect among others of the Berdiaevian work, on the other hand almost the entire voluminous book of Boris Mouravieff (1961–1965), *Gnôsis. Étude et commentaire sur la tradition ésotérique de l'orthodoxie orientale*, stood within the pale of esotericism. It is a big compendium of "psychosophy" (as he calls it) and of a Christian anthroposophy, partly Steinerian in character, that this independent thinker, also somewhat influenced by Gurdjieff, presents us in the form of instructions meant for the reader's illumination and inner transformation. All the same, the references to the Western corpus are rare in it. The Centre d'Études Chrétiennes Ésotériques created in 1961 by Mouravieff has enjoyed a certain success.

One of the most remarkable books of the twentieth century among all those mentioned in this chapter is *Méditations sur les 22 Arcanes majeurs du tarot*, written in French; published anonymously, first in German in 1972, then in several other languages (*Meditations on the Tarot: A Journey into Christian Hermeticism*, 1985). The author, Valentin Tomberg (1901–1973), a Russian of Baltic German origin, was a professor of law. He was a member of the Anthroposophical Society for a few years, but broke from it and spent the last years of his life in London where he wrote this work. There may not be a better introduction to Christian theosophy and to any philosophical reflection on Western esoteric currents. Let us note that despite the title, it is hardly a treatise on the Tarot (the author uses the Arcana only as a point of departure, a support, for "meditation").

In France, Auguste-Edouard Chauvet, a continuator of Fabre d'Olivet amd of Saint-Yves d'Alveydre (chapter 4, section II, 3), scrutinized the book of Moses, taking support from his two predecessors, but enriched their contribution with new perspectives; his *Ésotérisme de la Genèse* (1946–1948) was one of the most interesting works of Christian theosophy in the twentieth century. Robert Amadou, who considered himself the disciple of Chauvet, was his commentator and appeared as a Christian theosopher (*Occident, Orient: parcours d'une tradition*, 1987; and cf. *supra*, introduction, section III).

The work of the Islamologist Henry Corbin dealt primarily with the theosophies of Islam, but occasionally with Christian theosophy, marshalled in the context of the three great monotheisms. Translator and commentator of Iranian and Islamic philosophical texts, this university scholar attempted to ally scientific rigor with personal commitment to a theosophy whose Christian component takes on, in his work, a distinctly docetist hue. Making a plea for the constitution of a "comparative esotericism of the Religions of the Book," he sought to bring out the relationships that would connect some Christian theosophers (like Swedenborg and Oetinger) with their Shi'ite Islamic counterparts (cf. e.g., "Herméneutique spirituelle comparée," in *Eranos Jahrbuch*, no. 33, 1965). In the work of this exegete, Sophia and the angelic world occupy an important position. Prominent too is what he called the *mundus imaginalis*—the imaginal world—or mesocosm, an intermediary world situated between the perceptible world and the "intelligible" or divine world, a *mundus* "where spirits become corporealized and bodies become spiritualized."

3. Gnosis and Science: Toward a New Pansophy?

The occultist current had shown itself powerless to stimulate the emergence of a new Nature philosophy comparable to the *Naturphilosophie* of the period of German Romanticism. The twentieth century did not really witness a resurgence of this type, despite the work of certain authors already encountered here, such as Rudolf Steiner, Frater Albertus, and Alexander von Bernus (section I, 3), who stood to some extent within this kind of tradition.

It is nevertheless appropriate to make a special place for Gurdjieff and for Ouspensky. The Greco-Armenian George Ivanovitch Gurdjieff (1877–1949; section II, 3), like Boehme but without connecting to theosophy of a Christian type, posited the existence of two Natures. One is "creatural"; the other is "eternal," a duality concretely manifested by the appearance of a great many levels of materiality within a network of universal interdependence. Structured according to an original arithmology, this cosmology, or this cosmosophy, is rich and complex. In *In Search of the Miraculous: Fragments of an Unknown Teaching* (1949), the Russian Piotr Dem'ianovich Ouspensky (section II, 3) explicated this philosophy of Gurdjieff, of which we also find elements in the book by the latter, *Beelzebub's Tales to his Grandson* (published in 1950). Ouspensky appeared furthermore in a good position beside Gurdjieff as a philosopher of Nature, by his book *A New Model of the Universe* (1930–1931, as well as *Tertium Organon*, 1920–1922, already cited in relation to Gurdjieff, chapter 4, section II, 3).

In the course of the last decades, new reflections were put forward, bearing on this idea of Nature philosophy understood in a light of *gnosis*. This was the case of thinkers such as, first, the perennialist Seyyed Hosseyn Nasr (*Man and Nature*, 1968; section II, 2) and second, the microphysicist Basarab Nicolescu (*Nous, la particule et le monde*, 1985; and this evocative title: *La science, le sens et l'évolution: essai sur J. Böhme*, 1988 [*Science, Meaning and Evolution: The Cosmology of Jacob Boehme*, 1991]). A third example is the philosopher Michel Cazenave (*La Science et l'Âme de Monde*, 1983). At this juncture, mention must be made of a great mind of our times, Raymond Abellio (1907–1986; section I, 1; III, 1), a graduate of the École Polytechnique. Highly educated in both the "hard sciences" and the humanities, this philosopher has authored many writings on Kabbalah, on astrology and on the Tarot. However, he is mostly renowned for having elaborated an "absolute structure" (cf. *La Structure absolue*, 1965) founded on the idea of "universal interdependence" and whose practical application is meant to lead to a form of *gnosis* both experiential and intellectual.

In the fields of physics, astrophysics, and life sciences, an increasing number of thinkers emerged, proposing models of the universe, suggesting hypotheses of meaning. The problem of the origins of the cosmos and that of the relationships between Spirit and Nature, were—and continue to be—the subject of passionate and impassioned debates. These take the form of many conferences and symposia (of the type "Science and Tradition," "Religion and Science," etc.), in which the names of the representatives of the esoteric currents of the past are sometimes convoked. These debates, however, nearly always result in considerations privileging the "hard sciences," even while claiming to rejoice in seeing the emergence of new paradigms that would free scientific research from the ghetto to which scienticism had confined it for many decades. From an esoteric perspective, such debates, at their best, tend to produce forms of *neo-gnosis* very different from those that had previously flourished (to wit, *La Gnose de Princeton* [1974] of Raymond Ruyer, *The Tao of Physics* [1975] of Fritjof Capra, or *L'Esprit cet inconnu* [1977] of Jean Charon). Indeed, what differentiates such *neo-gnosis* from most *gnostic* constructions presented in the earlier chapters is that the former borrow from the latter only some of their "exterior" characteristics, thus failing to be based on a "myth of origins." According to these former constructions, a spiritually conducted hermeneutic would be capable of approaching such a myth on a variety of levels of reality.

II. At the Crossroads of "Tradition"

1. René Guénon

To counteract the multiplicity of initiatic Orders connected with the occultist current and the aspects of the latter that he deemed doubtful, the Frenchman René Guénon (1886–1951) undertook a work of reformation placed under the sign of "Tradition." He knew these Orders well for having been a member of several of them in his youth. He had even flirted with spiritualism around 1908. In 1914, he took initiation into the Grand Lodge of France. Within the Gnostic Church (chapter 4, section III, 1), he frequented men (Léon Champrenaud and Albert de Pouvourville) whose influence on him, added to that of the Orientals whom he met in 1908 and 1909, determined his vocation as a reformer.

In 1921, he published *Introduction générale à l'étude des doctrines hindoues* (*Introduction to the Study of the Hindu Doctrines*)[1] in which the essence of his metaphysics is already expounded. In *Le Théosophisme. Histoire d'une pseudo-religion* (*Theosophy, the History of a Pseudo-Religion*), published the same year and directed against the Theosophical Society (TS), he demonstrated his biting, polemical turn of mind, which also animated *L'Erreur spirite* (1923 [*The Spiritist Fallacy*]), another poisoned arrow, shot this time against Spiritualism. Almost all his subsequent works reveal this will to cleanse, to purify, which bears not only on the Western esoteric currents (especially the occultist one), but just as much on most Western philosophies (*Orient and Occident*, 1924 [*East and West*]).

In 1927, in *Le Roi du Monde* (*King of the World*) he affirmed the existence of a spiritual center or "geometric space," guarantor of the orthodoxy of the different traditions. In *La Crise du Monde moderne* (1927 [*The Crisis of the Modern World*]), he compares the Hindu vision of the cosmic cycles with our current civilization, identifying the latter with the so-called era of the *Kali Yuga*, a dark age of degeneration coming at the end of one of the "great cycles" or *manvantaras*. In 1930, Guénon traveled to Egypt where he remained until his death, occurring at his home in Cairo. There he wrote *Le Symbolisme de la Croix* (1931 [*The Symbolism of the Cross*]), *Les États multiples de l'Être* (1932 [*The Multiple States of the Being*]), *Le Règne de la quantité et les signes des temps* (1945 [*The Reign of Quantity and the Signs of the Times*]), and *La Grande Triade* (1946 [*The Great Triad*]). His abundant bibliography is not limited to these titles. He has always proved furthermore, to be a prolific author of articles, an indefatigable correspondent, and a polemicist with an acid pen.

Guénon claimed to possess a complex metaphysical doctrine of Hindu origin bearing on the Non-Being (Brahma, the Absolute) and the Being—His manifestation—with "multiple states," to which human beings are connected. This metaphysics is absent from the Western esoteric currents. Guénon nevertheless occupies an important place in their history, for four main reasons. The first is his numerous

---

1. All the works cited here were published in English by Sophia Perennis in 2004/2005.

public stands: he attracted much attention by making strong pro-
nouncements. The second is the insistence with which he affirmed
the existence of a "primordial Tradition" situated beyond all these
currents and all the traditions and religions of the world. Guénon
received the heritage of this notion from the Renaissance (*philosophia
perennis*), from Romanticism, and from the TS, but he hypostasized
it more than anyone else hitherto had done. Furthermore, he insisted
on the need for authentic initiatic filiation in the attempt to gain
access to this "Tradition," an insistence well adapted to inciting the
members of many existing initiatic societies to question this Tradition's
value. Third, he produced many writings on symbolism, an area of
predilection for anyone who feels at home with various forms of "esotericism"—even if the manner in which he theorizes the notion of
"symbol" can leave demanding readers dissatisfied. Fourth, his writing
style is remarkably clear and convincing, in harmony with the vigor of
the purpose (even though the latter lacks historical rigor); this partly
accounts for the influence he has been exerting from the 1920s until
today in various milieux—philosophical, literary, and artistic.

To oppose the proliferation of initiations of his time, which
he considered false for the most part, Guénon proposed the initiatic regularity of Freemasonry and of the Catholic Church. However,
this regularity is only a temporary channel; Christianity itself must be
transcended, because any religion is only a form, a limiting aspect of
the "supreme intellectuality," an avatar of the primordial Tradition.
Guénon represents an impressive voice of intellectual asceticism. No
one more than he has striven to put us on guard against the confu-
sion between the "mental" and the "spiritual," and against sentimen-
tality in matters of spirituality. "Esotericism," or better "esoterism"
(cf. introduction, section I), often takes, in Guénon, the meaning
of "metaphysical principles," whereas "exotericism" covers everything
that relates to the "individual."

It remains, nevertheless, that this "Descartes of esotericism,"
whose power of synthesis we can only admire, blithely threw the
baby out with the bathwater. While rejecting Western philosophy,
he seemed to know precious little about Christian theosophy (the
Germanic world was alien to him). By mistrust of the adulterated,
he preserved nothing, or nearly, of the hermetic-alchemical Western

tradition and located at the Renaissance the great divorce from meta-physics. Through ignorance of the epistemological breakthroughs of his time, he had a false—because outdated—idea of science (indeed, he was neither a scientist nor a full-fledged historian). He rejected this science, just as he condemned modernity in all its aspects—and loftily ignored Nature. The "world of manifestation"—the palpable world—as he liked to say, has even less reality than our shadow projected on a wall. Because of their lack of interest in Nature and most Western esoteric traditions, within the history of the latter, "Guénonism," and perennialism in general, constitute a new phenomenon.

2. The Perennialist Current

Perennialism (from the Latin *philosophia perennis*) serves to designate (see also introduction, section I) a religious philosophy that empha-sizes the notion of primordial Tradition, mother of all the others and understood in a Guénonian sense. If Guénon is, in some way, its leader, his principal "successor" was Frithjof Schuon (1907–1999; *De l'Unité transcendante des religions*, 1948 [*The Transcendent Unity of Reli-gion*, 1953]; *L'Ésotérisme comme principe et comme voie*, 1978 [*Esoterism as Principle and as Way*, 1981], *Sur les traces de la religion pérenne*, 1982 [*Echoes of Perennial Wisdom*, 1992], etc.). Schuon, a Swiss established in the United States in 1981, has exerted and is still exerting an influence extending to a very wide audience.

In the wake of Guénon and of Schuon (but certain notable dif-ferences separate them) a few personalities stand out. Among them are, in France, Constant Chevillon, an important figure of Martinism and of Freemasonry (*La Tradition universelle*, 1946); Leo Schaya (*La Création en Dieu*, 1983), and the philosopher Georges Vallin (La Per-spective métaphysique, 1977). We also find Catholics nevertheless very close to Guénonian thought (Louis Charbonneau-Lassay, *Le Bestiaire du Christ*, 1940 [*The Bestiary of Christ*]), and Jean Borella, *Esotérisme guénonien et mystère chrétien*, 1998 [*Guénonian Esoterism and Christian Mystery*]).

In Italy, Julius Evola's (section I, 1) work has been the subject of a great many commentaries since the early 1990s. In England, it was Martin Lings (*The Eleventh Hour*, 1987), who was Guénon's personal secretary. In the United States, we find the academics Ananda K. Coomaraswamy (1877–1947), prolific author of writings on various religions, Seyyed Hosseyn Nasr (*The Encounter of Man and Nature*, 1968; *Knowledge and the Sacred*, 1981; section I, 3), Huston Smith (*The Religions of Man*, 1958; *Forgotten Truth*, 1976; *Beyond the Post-Modern Mind*, 1982), and James Cutsinger, author of many articles since the 1980s and one of the principal commentators of Schuonian thought. The differences of orientation among these perennialists go beyond the scope of this short presentation (e.g., considerations on Nature feature prominently in Nasr's philosophy). Many journals, associations, and study centers also represent this current.

3. Initiatic Societies

Among the masonic Rites already mentioned, Rectified Scottish Rite, Ancient and Accepted Scottish Rite, and Memphis-Misraïm have survived since World War I. In the paramasonic domain properly speaking, Martinism has fragmented into several Orders with a complex history and in which, depending on the branch, the ritual of the times of Papus, and even the theurgical rite of the Élus Coëns are still practiced. The Brethern of the Societas Rosicruciana in Anglia (SRIA), limited, as we have seen (chapters 4, section III, 1), to regular masons, pursue an initiatic work of a neo-Rosicrucian type behind the discreet cover of their Lodges or so-called "Colleges." Issued from the SRIA, the Golden Dawn (GD) disappeared at the beginning of the century, at least in its original form. The Order of the Builders of the Adytum founded by Paul Foster Case constitutes a sort of extension of it; Hermeticism, Kabbalah, and Tarot are part of its subjects of study. The Ordo Templi Orientis (chapter 4, section III, 1) developed greatly, especially in the United States, with an important center in California.

The symbol of the rose and the cross has been, in the twentieth century, the object of considerable interest, which broadly exceeded the boundaries of paramasonry. Created in 1915 by Harvey Spencer Lewis, the Antiquus Mysticus Ordo Rosae Crucis already counted a few hundred thousand members at the death of its founder. Quantitatively, it is, after the TS, the second most important movement in the history of Western esotericism proper. Open to the outer world and to modernity, it provides its members with a culture (many lectures, site visits, libraries, etc.) as well as with an initiatic way. Its headquarters, originally located in the great "Amorcian" center of San José, California, moved to Omonville in France in 1990. Very different is the Lectorium Rosicrucianum (or International School of the Golden Rosycross), founded in Haarlem, the Netherlands, in 1924 by Jan van Rijckenborgh (*alias* Jan Leene) and of which an important center is located in Ussat-les-Bains, France. Its teaching is of a Gnostic (in the sense of ancient Gnosticism) and Cathar type, rather difficult to blend with traditional Rosicrucianism (of the seventeenth century); this is, however, what the thinkers of the Lectorium have been attempting to do. Among the many neo-Rosicrucian Orders, let us further mention the Fraternità Terapeutica Magica di Myriam, in Italy, created by Ciro Formisano (*alias* Giuliano Kremmerz; his *Corpus Philosophorum totius Magiae* was published in 1988–1989). This Order has a partly therapeutic vocation. It combines Rosicrucianism with egyptophilia and, since its founder's death, has enjoyed a certain success. This list of so-called Rosicrucian Orders is not exhaustive (the most complete listing is found in the book by Massimo Introvigne, *Il Cappello del Mago*, 1990).

The Anthroposophical Society (chapter 4, section II, 3), which became Allgemeine Anthrosophische Gesellschaft in 1923, has maintained an intense activity undiminished by the death of its founder, Rudolf Steiner. Dornach has remained, as before, a high place of culture and a center whose influence was favored by the success of Steiner schools for children (the first "Freie Waldorfschule" was created in Stuttgart in 1919). The same goes for the TS, whose centers remain very active in the countries where it has taken hold. Its branches, however, are varied, and some of them separated from it to constitute original organizations. One example is the Loge Mystique Chrétienne (LMC; close in spirit to Anna Kingsford, cf. chapter, 4, section II, 2), founded in 1923 by the psychoanalyst Violet Mary Firth (*alias* Dion Fortune, who came from the GD); this LMC became in 1928 the Society of the Inner Light, which practiced various forms of evocatory magic.

In addition to these formally constituted associations are various forms of "Fraternities," "Fellowships," and esoteric study groups. Thus,

Gurdjieff (section I, 3), established in France in 1922, founded his "Priory" in Avon and in 1933 settled definitively in Paris. In 1915, he met Ouspensky (section I, 3), to whom we owe a detailed relation of the master's words as well as the "work" practiced in the "Gurdjieff groups." This "work" rests on a sort of pedagogy of "awakening" (cf. *In Search of the Miraculous: Fragments of an Unknown Teaching*, 1949; section I, 3). Gurdjieff groups still operate in various countries.

The very eclectic Universal Great Brotherhood of Serge Raynaud de la Ferrière, begun in 1947, active especially in Central and South America, combines purportedly "pre-Columbian" teachings with speculations on the Age of Aquarius. It is a popular movement, like the New Acropolis (NA), founded in the 1950s by the Argentinian Angel Livraga. Established in many countries, in France by Fernand Schwartz, the NA provides courses and publishes periodicals about the various religious traditions of humanity, notably their artistic aspects. In 1952, the Colombian Samael Aun Weor founded a Gnostic Association of Anthropological and Cultural Studies, it too very eclectic, which mixes Buddhism, Tantrism, Steinerian anthroposophy, sexual alchemy, and the teachings of Gurdjieff. Let us finally mention the Atlantis Association and the journal by the same name, founded in 1927 by Paul Le Cour—one of the first in France to launch the idea of an Age of Aquarius. It is characterized by a Christian esotericism of an eclectic bent in which, as its name indicates, the myth of Atlantis holds an important place.

4. "Tradition": A Multifaceted Notion

To the various associations just discussed, we could add a few more, most of which would rather belong to what is called the New Religious Movements (NMR). The NMR represents a phenomenon that began to manifest itself in the 1960s. Many are those whose teaching contains elements of an esoteric type in the sense that we understand it (e.g., the Universal White Brotherhood of Peter Konstantinov Deunov and Mikhaël Omraam Aïvanhov). The same goes for the literature of the New Age, which to a certain extent feeds on such elements. New Age is the general term for a diffuse movement that has prospered from its beginnings in California in the 1970s, and one of whose origins goes back partly to Alice Bailey. This founder of the Arcane School in 1923 is also the author of many works of occultist content. The supporters of the New Age proclaim the coming of a new era, the Age of Aquarius, characterized by a progress of humanity placed under the sign of a rediscovered harmony and of an "enlarged (extended) consciousness."

Part of the panoply of the New Age is the practice of "channeling." This consists in letting speak, through a medium, entities from the beyond, who, unlike what is supposed to happen in Spiritualism, are not deceased persons. One of the first examples of channeling is that (in the 1930s, in Zurich) of messages coming from an entity giving itself the name Atma. The entity expressed itself during séances organized for this purpose (and in which Carl Gustav Jung happened to take part), through the voice of a "sleeping" (nonmagneticized) subject, Oscar Rudolf Schlag, a person well learned in terms of esoteric currents. The speeches of Atma, published in several volumes (*Die Lehren des A.*, 1995–2010), contain a wealth of passages in an oracular style on alchemy, the tarot, magic, arithmology, mythology, and Hindu traditions (on yoga, notably) as well. More recently, channeling has been part of the panoply of the New Age.

On the shores of this oceanic landscape constituted by the New Age and the NRM, the esoteric currents properly speaking lose their outlines. They also dissolve into what is called the Cultic Milieu (a felicitous expression introduced by Colin Campbell in 1972), which consists, for example, of "occultist fairs." These are actual marketplaces, such as the Kohoutek Celebration of Consciousness in San Francisco in January 1974, an improbable jumble where all the imaginable fringe sciences were on display in stands and booths. This was only one of the first major manifestations of this type, in a long series that is ongoing. What is essential here, on the one hand, seems to be the need for "transformation" motivating the participants, and, on the other hand, the opportunity to discover their good grain under the chaff for those who want to sift through it.

The world of publishing provides group fairs of another type. The year 1960 saw the publication in France of a book typical in this regard, signed by Louis Pauwels and Jacques Bergier (*Le Matin des magiciens.* [*The Morning of the Magicians,* 1963]), which quickly appeared in several languages. In this skillful commercial enterprise, whose success was extended by the magazine *Planète* (1961–1968), the metaphysical and religious mysteries are presented as scientific enigmas, and vice versa.

III. Arts and Humanities

I. Arts and Literature

The prose and poetry of Oscar Vadislas Milosz (*Ars Magna*, 1924; *Les Arcanes*, 1927) are the work of an "initiate" and a great artist. The Russian Alexander Blok ("The Rose and the Cross," 1915) is close to him in many ways. In the work of the Portuguese Fernando Pessoa, elements borrowed from the esoteric currents often mold his poetry and short prose pieces (thus, *A Hora do Diablo*, 1931–1932). The Surrealists (André Breton, *Arcane 17*, 1947; *L'Art magique*, 1957) drew from the corpus of the "occult sciences." However, personal involvement is more explicit among the young authors of the movement called "Le Grand Jeu" and the journal by the same name (1928–1931), which in the 1920s flourished around René Daumal (cf. his book *Le Mont Analogue*, 1952, posthumous edition [*Mount Analogue*, 2004]). They drew part of their inspiration from the said currents.

This involvement is also explicit in a number of works of fiction. Thus in the novels of Gustav Meyrink (*Der Golem*, 1915; *Das Grüne Gesicht*, 1916, etc.) and of Mircea Eliade (*infra*, 2; his novel *Viata noua*, 1941; his short story *The Secret of Dr. Honigberger* [1940] was published in 1999). Eliade was not only a famous historian of religions but also a novelist. Personal commitment is less conspicuous in Hermann Hesse's *Das Glasperlenspiel*, 1943 (*The Glass Bead Game*, 1970). The English-speaking world is especially rich in "fantastic" works of fiction: the novels of Charles Williams (*War in Heaven*, 1930; *The Greater Trumps*, 1933) and those of Dion Fortune (*The Secrets of Dr. Traverner*, 1926) also indeed belong to the esoteric currents. Later, the Frenchman Raymond Abellio (section I, 1, 3) attempted to communicate the essence of his *gnosis* in his own novels (e.g., *Les Yeux d'Ézéchiel sont ouverts*, 1949; *La Fosse de Babel*, 1962).

Dan Brown's *The Da Vinci Code* (2003) well reflects the interest of a broad public inclined toward the "conspiracy theories" so popular today, whereas Umberto Eco's *Il Pendolo di Foucault* (1988), which parodies these famous "theories" in a mischievous fashion, is not meant to deliver any message whatsoever. In this mischievous genre, spiced with a touch of the picaresque, also appeared works of fiction by Frederick Tristan, for example, *Les Tribulations héroïques de Balthasar Kober* (1980).

In the plastic arts, the very figurative paintings in the last manner of the Portuguese painter Lima de Frietas suggest possible connections with Surrealism. However, they are actually very distinct from this current by their elaborately developed neo-Pythagoreanism and their explicit references to esoteric themes, for example, to seventeenth-century Rosicrucianism ("Calmo na falsa morte," 1985; "O Jardim dos Hespérides," 1986; etc.). The influence of the TS proved deep and lasting (cf. the fine retrospective *The Spiritual in Art: Abstract Painting, 1890–1985*, 1986, and *Okkultismus und Avantgarde. Von Munch bis Mondrian, 1900–1915*, 1995). In the work of the German Joseph Anton Schneiderfranken (*alias* Bô-Yin-Râ), a poet and spiritual master, painting and writing draw their inspiration from an orientalizing esotericism (*Das Buch der Gespräche*, 1920) [*The Book of Dialogues*]. In architecture, let us recall that the Goetheanum (chapter 4, section III, 3), at Dornach, near Basle, designed by Rudolf Steiner, was reconstructed after the fire of 1922 and that its stained-glass windows reflect a very "anthroposophical" symbolism.

Among the many Tarot decks of the century, several demonstrate an attempt toward figurative renewal in the tradition of fin de siècle occultism. Thus, "Cartomancia Lusso"; "Rider-Waite Tarot" (1909) of Pamela Coleman Smith; "Thot Tarot," toward 1940, of Frieda Harris, inspired by *The Book of Thoth*, 1944 of Aleister Crowley (section I, 1; chapter 4, section III, 1)—a deck that has become one of the most famous Tarots in the world. The art, also very figurative, of the color plates and illustrations for Anglo-Saxon books where Art Nouveau and neo-Romanticism are combined in an original fashion, features a specific genre that deserves study (thus, the large in-folio volume by Manly Palmer Hall, *The Secret Teachings of all Ages*, 1928).

It would be difficult to discuss musical esotericism other than with respect to the theories expounded by composers (but when such theories exist, we can expect to find their traces in the scores). Examples are Cyril Scott (*The Infuence of Music*, 1933) or Karlheinz Stockhausen (*Texte zur Musik*, 1970–1977). For the same reason, there would be little to say about cinema, which makes use of themes or of motifs that, although present in the esoteric currents, are not unique to them (cf. introduction, sections I and IV). On the other hand, the seventh art lends itself admirably to the genre of fantasy as well as to the fantastic. However, cinema sometimes resorts to explicit references to certain characters or traditions—thus, *Meetings with Remarkable Men*, by Peter Brook (1978), more especially because this feature draws inspiration from Gurdjieff.

2. Psychology and the Humanities

The thought of Sigmund Freud has deep roots in the romantic *Naturphilosophie* that discovered the existence of the unconscious (chapter 4, I, 1), but it goes to the psychologist Herbert Silberer to have been the first to suggest a psychoanalytical reading of the alchemical texts (*Probleme der Mystik und ihrer Symbolik*, 1914). It is, however, to Carl Gustav Jung (1875–1961) that is due the title of great explorer of some of the "psychological" riches of part of the modern Western alchemical corpus. He wanted to demonstrate (*Psychologie und Alchemie*, 1936–1952; *Mysterium Conjunctionis*, 1955–1956; etc.) that "transmutation" and the symbolism of the stages of its journey correspond to a highly positive work of the psyche in search of its own edification or harmonization, of its "individuation." With this in mind, he selected from this corpus the titles the most likely to support his demonstrations, and in making this choice he underwent the influence of the representatives of Occultism—a current from which he was not very distant chronologically and with which he was well familiar. Now, Jung had tended to present alchemy as a whole as a sort of spiritual technique (cf. e.g., M. A. Atwood, in chaper 4, section I, 4), thereby underplaying the properly "scientific" aim of most of the alchemists (cf. chapter 2, section III, 2). Thus, he contributed to give a partial idea of the history of alchemy—but in stimulating public interest in this genre of literature, he simultaneously contributed to "repatriate" it into our culture.

Some philosophers have pursued a rather similar direction, by introducing the Western esoteric corpus into the field of their reflections. This pursuit can lead philosophy back to its vocation of a spiritual exigency, indeed of a transmutative practice of being (as in Françoise Bonardel, *Philosophie de l'alchimie. Grand Oeuvre et modernité*, 1993). Alternatively, it can open the classical logics to new approaches (thus Jean-Jacques Wunenberger, *La Raison contradictoire*, 1990). It can place the esoteric *imaginaire* in the perspective of a so-called "traditional" anthropology (Gilbert Durand, *Sciences de l'Homme et Tradition*, 1975). Again, it can marry metaphysics, esotericism, and psychology (Robert J. W. Evans, *Imaginal Body*, 1982; *The New Gnosis*, 1984).

Indeed, embedded in a universe considered bereft of consciousness and in a human community henceforth lacking any ideologies or even ideals, modern men and women often feel as though they are confronted with themselves in isolation. They are therefore easily tempted to see in certain elements of Western esotericism an approach to self-knowledge, which would not depend on previous adherence to a system of beliefs or of ethics, but which, they think, might be capable of conferring meaning on their life and on the universe. The *Oratio* of Pico della Mirandola on the "dignity of the human being" (chapter 2, section I, 3) has thus become topical once again, in the sense that it would be our responsibility always to redefine ourselves, to find or to rediscover our place in Nature and within a universal society and culture.

If this tendency does indeed lie within the spirit of the New Age, it nevertheless goes beyond it, by taking the form of a hitherto unparalleled interest in psychology. Since the mid-twentieth century, we have been experiencing a "psychological" epoch (i.e., one in which people are keenly interested in various forms of psychological techniques). Elements of Western esotericism thus penetrate, accompanied by borrowings from various Eastern "wisdoms," into the general public through the channel of therapies, whence the success of a Carl Gustav Jung—or of a John G. Bennett (*Gurdjieff: Meeting a New World*, 1973). Bennett could transpose into clear language the abstruse statements of Gurdjieff, whose teachings also belong, after all, to a form of therapy. Whence also, outside the "psychological" field, we witness the success of a Mircea Eliade (*supra*, 1), historian of religions whose work responds well to a double demand for culture and universality, and who strove to show that the "sacred" is a constitutive element of human nature. This idea is debatable, certainly, but it incited him to prospect the history of the religious traditions of the world, including—although in a rather limited scope—that of the esoteric currents in the West (*A History of Religious Ideas*, 1976–1983; *Occultism, Witchcraft, and Cultural Fashion*, 1976).

3. Historiography of Western Esotericism

As stated in the introduction (sections III and IV), it is appropriate to distinguish two categories of historians; on the one hand, the "generalists"; on the other hand, those who confine themselves to the study of specific authors or currents. Of course, some are both at once.

For a list of those representatives of the first category who strive to refine the methods of approaching the specialty considered as such, we simply refer to the introduction. Let us cite here some other "generalists," whose main purpose is nevertheless not especially in the order of methodology proper. Karl R. H. Frick, author of *Licht und Finsternis* and *Die Erleuchteten* (1973–1978), has been dealing especially with esoteric societies. James Webb (*The Occult Underground*, 1974; *The Occult Establishment*, 1976) has clarified various aspects of the occultist current and its repercussions over the past about one hundred and fifty years. J. Gordon Melton has edited a useful encyclopedia (*Occultism and Parapsychology*, 2001). Massimo Introvigne (a specialist, as is Melton, of the NRM) has given the best study of all the "magical" (in the broad sense) currents and societies of the West having existed since the middle of the nineteenth century (*Il Cappello del Mago*, 1990). Finally yet importantly, Joscelyn Godwin continues to pursue a variety of researches. Professor of musicology, Godwin is the author of *Harmonies of Heaven and Earth* (1987), *L'Ésotérisme musical en France* (1991), and so on, and in addition has to his credit a wide range of publications on many authors—on Robert Fludd, Athanasius Kircher, "fin de siècle" esotericism, and the like (cf. notably his important work *The Theosophical Enlightenment*, 1994).

As recalled above, the second category includes (here again, since the mid-twentieth century) historians whose works pertain to one or several authors. Its representatives are too numerous to be the object of a list, even a succinct one; but attention is called to the first lines of the bibliography presented in this volume, which refers to a bibliography both general and particular.

Let us add in closing that students of "Western esotericism" are aided in their research by the existence of some specialized and richly documented periodicals. Their titles appear *infra*, in the *addenda* of the bibliography. Also included in these *addenda* are the names of the best libraries dedicated to this same specialty.

Bibliography

This bibliography contains only a few titles selected from among historical and critical works of a general character, published since 1964. For a detailed bibliography (through 2000) pertaining to particular authors or currents, cf. *infra*, our work *Accès de l'ésotérisme occidental*, vol. 2. pp. 371–414, and addenda in its English translation: *Theosophy, Imagination, Tradition*, pp. 249–259.

Bogdan Henrik, *Western Esotericism and Rituals of Initiation*, Albany (NY), State University of New York Press (SUNY Series in Western Esoteric Traditions), 2007 (1st ed., 2003, titled *From Darkness to Light. Western Esoteric Rituals of Initiation*). Insightful study bearing on the relationships between rites and initiatic societies of an esoteric type (modern West). French translation 2010 (Paris, Edidit).

Brach Jean-Pierre, *La Symbolique des nombres*, Paris, Presses Universitaires de France (Que Sais-Je?), 1995. Expanded version, *Il Simbolismo dei numeri*, Rome, Aekekios, 1999. While presenting the history of arithmosophy in the West, the author also furnishes time-pertinent surveys on several esoteric currents.

Bonardel Françoise, *L'Hermétisme*, Paris, Presses Universitaires de France (Que Sais-Je?), 2002 (revised and expanded edition; 1st ed., 1985). In fact, by "hermetism" the author means a general field extending beyond that of neo-Alexandrian Hermetism and that of alchemy. This is a historical albeit rather personal approach to the subject.

(Le) Défi magique, Massimo Introvigne and Jean Baptiste Martin (ed.), vol. 1: *Ésotérisme, occultisme, spiritisme*, Lyon, Presses Universitaires de Lyon I, 1994 (Proceedings of the international conference held in Lyons in April 1992). Contains interesting contributions, both on specific points and on methodology.

Dictionary of Gnosis and Western Esotericism, J. W. Hanegraaff, A. Faivre, J.-P. Brach, R. van den Broek (ed.), 2 vol., Leyden, E. J. Brill, 2005. This is certainly the most indispensable work of the entire list. Written by some 180 collaborators, it covers the historical field of Western esotericism from late Antiquity to the present.

Dictionnaire critique de l'ésotérisme, Jean Servier (ed.), Paris, Presses Universitaires de France, 1998. The editor intended to devote this dictionary to a sort of "universal esotericism,," dividing it into "sectors" of which the whole is supposed to relate to almost all the cultures of the world. Let us nevertheless mention the presence of the sector "Modern Western esotericism," whose contents correspond, essentially, to the main purpose of the present book.

Epochen der Naturmystik, Antoine Faivre and Rolf Christian Zimmermann (ed.), Berlin, Erich Schmidt, 1979. This book treats the Nature philosophies in the context of the modern Western esoteric currents.

Ésotérisme, gnoses et imaginaire symbolique (Mélanges offerts à Antoine Faivre), Richard Caron, Joscelyn Godwin, Wouter J. Hanegraaff, Jean-Louis Vieillard-Baron (ed.), Louvain, Peeters (Gnostica. Texts and Interpretations), 2001. This collective work is recommended as much for its contributions on specific currents as for those on questions of methodology.

Études d'histoire de l'ésotérisme (Mélanges offerts à Jean-Pierre Laurant), Jean-Pierre Brach and Jérôme Rousse-Lacordaire (ed.), Paris, Le Cerf, 2007. Fine collection of articles.

Faivre Antoine, *Accès de l'ésotérisme occidental*, 2 vols., Paris, Gallimard (Bibliothèque des sciences humaines), 1996. Contains various historical and methodological studies on the subject, both specific and general. English translation: *Access to Western Esotericism*, Albany (NY), State University of New York Press (SUNY Series in Western Esoteric Traditions), 1996, for vol. 1; and *Theosophy, Imagination, Tradition*, trans. Christine Rhone, (same publisher), 2000, for vol. 2.

Form e correnti dell' esoterismo occidentale, Alessandro Grossato (ed.), Venice, Medusa /Fundazione Giorgio Cini, 2008. Proceedings of the international conference held in Venice in October 2007. Besides its interest with regard to specific currents, this collective work contains important, up-to-date contributions in methodology.

Frick Karl R. H., *Die Erleuchteten*, 3 vol., Graz, Ak. Druck- und Verlagsanstalt, 1973, 1975, 1978. Very well documented particularly for what concerns the Western societies (masonic, paramasonic, etc.) of an esoteric nature.

Gnosis and Hermeticism from Antiquity to Modern Times, Roelof Van den Broek and Wouter J. Hanegraaff (ed.), Albany (NY), State University of New York Press, 1998. Proceedings of the international conference held in Amsterdam in August 1994. One of the very first important collective works published, pertaining specifically to the specialty.

Godwin Joscelyn, *The Theosophical Enlightenment*, Albany (NY), State University of New York Press (SUNY Series in Western Esoteric Traditions), 1994. Fundamental work for what concerns certain major representatives of the Western esoteric currents, notably of the eighteenth and nineteenth centuries.

Goodrick-Clarke Nicholas, *The Western Esoteric Traditions. A Historical Introduction*, New York, Oxford University Press, 2008. A most valuable presentation of the main Western esoteric currents, which keeps abreast with the current state of research.

Hammer Olav, *Claiming Knowledge. Strategies of Epistemology from Theosophy to the New Age*, Leyden, E. J. Brill (Numen Book Series. Studies in the History of Religions), 2001. One of the most recent fundamental works on certain major contemporary Western esoteric currents, notably in their relations with the "New Age."

Hanegraaff Wouter J., *New Age Religion and Western Culture: Esotericism in the Mirror of Secular Thought*, Leyden, E. J. Brill, 1996 (and Albany (NY), State University of New York Press, 1998. A fundamental work on the historical and methodological levels, bearing not only on the relationships between the "New Age" and the modern Western esoteric currents, but also on the history of both.

Introvigne Massimo, *Il Cappello del mago*, Milan, Sugarco, 1990. An indispensable mine of information.

Laurant Jean-Pierre, *L'Ésotérisme chrétien en France au XIXe siècle*, Lausanne, L'Âge d'homme, 1992. A rather complete panorama of the question.

———, *L'Ésotérisme*, Paris, Cerf, 1993. An interesting synthetic approach.

Magic, Alchemy and Science, 15th–18th Centuries. The Influence of Hermes Trismegistus, Carlos Gilly and Cis van Hertum (ed.), 2 vol., Amsterdam, Centro Di (Bibliotheca Philosophica Hermetica), 2002. Each of the contributions is presented in two languages (Italian and English). To an impressive survey of scholarship comes to be added one of the best selections of illustrations ever presented.

Miers E. Horst, *Lexicon des Geheimwissens*, Munich, Wilhelm Goldmann, 1993. Well documented and very practical little dictionary.

Modern Esoteric Spirituality, Antoine Faivre and Jacob Needleman (ed.) (Associate Editor, Karen Voss), New York, Crossroad, 1992 (World Spirituality. An Encyclopedic History of the Religious Quest). An anthology of contributions each of which concerns a particular Western esoteric current.

Pasi Marco, *La Notion de magie dans le courant occultiste en Angleterre (1875–1947)*, 2004 (Thesis in presented at the E.P.H.E., Religious

Studies, Sorbonne). Besides a remarkable historical account of the said current, this work offers a major methodological contribution concerning notions such as "magic," "occultism," and the like.

Polemical Encounters. Esoteric Discourse and Its Others, Olav Hammer and Kocku von Stuckrad, ed., Leyden/Boston, E. J. Brill Academic Publishers (*Aries* Book Series. Texts and Studies in Western Esotericism), 2007. This collective volume engages the polemical structures that underlie both the identities within and the controversy about esoteric currents in European history.

Riffard Pierre, *L'Ésotérisme, Qu'est-ce que l'ésotérisme? Anthologie de l'ésotérisme occidental*, Paris, R. Laffont, 1990. Although debatable on the methodological level, contains an interesting selection of texts.

Stuckrad Kocku von, *Was ist Esoterik? Kleine Geschichte des geheimen Wissens*, Munich, C. H. Beck, 2004. English edition, *Western Esotericism. A History of Secret Knowledge*, London, Equinox, 2005. Original approach, interesting by the very nature of the author's methodological positions, which can nevertheless seem debatable.

Webb James, *The Occult Underground*, La Salle (Ill.), Open Court, 1974. Important concerning certain trends and major representatives of the esoteric currents of the nineteenth and twentieth centuries principally.

———, *The Occult Establishment* (same publisher), 1976. Same remarks.

Western Esotericism and the Science of Religion, Antoine Faivre and Wouter J. Hanegraaff (ed.), Louvain, Peeters (Gnostika. Texts and Interpretations), 1998 (Proceedings of the international conference of the International Association for the History of Religions (IAHR) held in Mexico City in 1995). This collective work is recommended not only for its contributions relating to some esoteric currents, but also mostly for those relating to questions of methodology.

Yates Frances A., *Giordano Bruno and the Hermetic Tradition*, London, Routledge & Kegan Paul, 1964. Several re-editions. This book still gives rise to many commentaries about the author's interpretations, but it remains fundamental concerning the study and the understanding of both the principal esoteric currents in the Renaissance era and some of their repercussions. It has contributed to the growth of the specialty on the academic plane.

Addenda

Current Periodicals of a Scholarly Character

Aries. The Journal of Western Esotericism, Antoine Faivre, Peter Forshaw, Nicholas Goodrick-Clarke and Wouter J. Hanegraaff (ed.). Biannual, in four languages. Leyden, E. J. Brill, since 2001 (previously, from 1985 to 2000: *Aries*, issues available from Ed. Archè-Edidit, in Paris).

Esoterica. The Journal of Hermetic Studies, Arthur Versluis (ed.), published online only (www.esoteric.msu.edu). Since 1999. Presents many contributions of both a general and a particular nature.

Chrysopoeia, Didier Kahn and Sylvain Matton (ed.), Paris, Archè—J. C. Bailly. Published irregularly, since 1987, in the form of often very copious volumes. This series is devoted to alchemy, but many contributions go beyond the scope of that specific field.

Gnostika, Hans Thomas Hakl (ed.), Sinzheim (Germany), AAWG. Quarterly. Published since 1996. Presents, on the one hand, rare or hard-to-find texts; on the other hand, a generous section dedicated to recent publications, conferences, symposia, and various activities relevant to the specialty.

Politica Hermetica, Jean-Pierre Laurant, Jean-Pierre Brach, etc. (ed.), Lausanne, L'Âge d'homme. Annual. Published since 1987. In principle dedicated to the relationships between politics and esotericism, but its contents extend broadly to other aspects of the latter.

Theosophical History, James A. Santucci (ed.), Fullerton (Cal.), California State University. Quarterly. Published since 1985. In principle dedicated to the history of the Theosophical Society, but its contents go beyond this scope to other currents and movements of an esoteric nature.

Specialized Libraries

Bibliotheca Philosophica Hermetica, in Amsterdam. Cf. site www.ritman library.nl/.

CESNUR (Center for Studies on New Religions), in Turin. Cf. site http://www.cesnur.org/.

Bibliothek Oscar R. Schlag, in Zurich. Cf., in the site www.zb.unizh. ch/, the heading "Spezialsammlungen," and inside the latter the subheading "Bibliothek Oskar R. Schlag."

Warburg Institute, in London. Cf. site http://warburg.sas.ac.ub.

Index of Names

Blavatsky, Helena Petrovna, 78, 86
Blok, Alexander, 104
Böcklin, Arnold, 88
Boehme, Jacob, 41–43, 50–53, 55, 56, 58, 67, 71, 73, 92, 93, 95
Bogdan, Henrik, 111
Bolos of Mendes, 26
Bonardel, Françoise, 107, 111
Bonatti, Guido, 30
Bonaventure (Saint), 14, 28
Borella, Jean, 99
Botticelli, 50
Bourignon, Antoinette, 43
Bovelles, Charles de -, 48
Bô-Yin-Râ, see Schneiderfranken, Anton
Brach, Jean-Pierre, 7, 16, 111, 112, 116
Brandler-Pracht, Karl, 89
Breton, André, 104
Britten, Emma Hardinge, 88
Brook, Peter, 106
Brook, Rulof van den -, 112, 113
Brothers, Richard, 60
Brown, Dan, 2, 105
Brucker, Jacob, 53
Bruno, Giordano, 10, 36, 47, 91
Buffon, Georges-Louis de- , 69
Bulgakov, Sergei, 92
Bulwer-Lytton, Edward G., 76, 84, 88
Bungus, Petrus, 48
Burton, Richard, 37

Caetano, Anselmo, 61
Cagliostro, see Balsamo, Joseph
Cahagnet, Louis-Alphonse, 73, 74
Calmet, Augustin, 59
Cambriel, 75
Camillo, Giulio, 48

Campanella, Tommaso, 4
Campbell, Colin, 103
Campbell, Joseph, 9
Canseliet, Eugène Léon, 90
Capelli, Ottavio, 65
Caron, Richard, 112
Carus, Carl Gustav, 72
Casaubon, Isaac, 36
Case, Paul Foster, 100
Castel, Louis-Bertrand, 59
Cazenave, Michel, 95
Cazotte, Jacques, 67
Cecco d'Ascoli, 30
Cellier, Léon, 76
Chamisso, Bravo, 49
Champier, Symphorien, 36
Champrenaud, Léon, 96
Charbonneau-Lassay, Louis, 99
Charcot, Jean-Martin, 62
Charles de Hesse-Cassel, see Karl von Hessen-Kassel
Charon, Jean, 96
Chastanier, Benedict, 66
Chauvet, Auguste-Edouard, 94
Chefdebien d'Armissan, François Marie, 66
Chennevière, Daniel, 89
Chevillon, Constant, 99
Chrétien de Troyes, 33
Clement of Alexandria, 27
Clement VII, 38
Clichtove, Josse, 48
Coeur, Jacques, see Jacques Coeur
Colberg, Daniel Ehregott, 53
Colonna, Francesco, 51
Comenius, Jan Amos, 45
Constant, Alphonse Louis, 74, 75, 80, 81
Coomaraswamy, 100
Copernicus, 37, 47

Corbin, Henry, 9, 73, 94
Cosimo de Medici, 35
Coudert, Allison, 17
Court de Gébelin, Antoine, 58
Croll, Oswald, 41
Crosbie, Robert, 87
Crowley, Aleister, 82, 85, 90, 91, 105
Cudworth, Ralph, 36
Cutsinger, James, 100
Cyliani, 75

Daneau, Lambert, 41
Dante, see Durante degli Alighieri
Dastin, John, 31
Daumal, René, 104
Davis, Andrew Jackson, 74, 79
Davis, Ferdinand, 74
Davy, Humphrey, 73
Dee, John, 36, 47
Delaage, Henri, 76
Denis, Ferdinand, 80
Deunov, Konstantinov, 102
Diderot, Denis, 60
Dion Fortune, see Firth, Violet Mary
Dionysius Aeropagita, 28, 47
Divish, Prokop, 62
Doinel, Jules, 86
Dorn, Gérard, 41, 49
Douzetemps, Melchior, 54
Drevon, Victor, 85
Durand, Gilbert, 9, 107
Durante degli Alighieri, 30, 88
Dutoit-Membrini, Jean-Philippe, 57

Eckartshausen, Karl von-, 56, 58, 59, 67
Ecker- und Eckhoffen, Hans Heinrich, 66

Eckhart (Meister Eckhart), see Hochheim, Eckhart von -
Eckleff, Karl Friedrich, 65
Eco, Umberto, 2, 105
Edighoffer, Roland, 45
Edward VI, 36
Eichhorn, Johann Gottfried, 1
Eliade, Mircea, 9, 104, 108
Encausse, Gérard, 81, 83–85
Ennemoser, Joseph, 72, 74
Erastus, Thomas, 41
Eschenbach, Wolfram von -, 33
Eschenmayer, Carl August von -, 71, 73
Esquiros, Alphonse, 75, 76
Etteilla, see Alliette
Everard, John, 36
Evans, J. W., 107
Evola, Julius, 91, 99

Fabre d'Olivet, Antoine, 58, 60, 74, 94
Fabré-Palaprat, Bernard-Raymond, 66
Fabricius, Johann Albert, 53
Faivre, Antoine, 16, 112, 114–116
Faucheux, Albert, 81
Faust, Georg, 48
Fechner, Gustav Theodor, 72, 76
Fende, Christian, 58
Ferdinand of Brunswick, see Ferdinand von Braunschweig
Ferdinand von Braunschweig, 64
Ferdinand II, 50
Ficino, Marsilio, 6, 23, 35, 38–40, 46, 47
Fictuld, Hermann, 61
Figuier, Louis, 80
Firth, Violet Mary, 101, 104
Flamel, Hortensius, 75

Flamel, Nicolas, 31
Florensky, Paul, 92
Fludd, Robert, 36, 38, 45, 46, 48, 51, 108
Foix-Candale, François, 36
Formisano, Giulio, see Kremmerz, Giuliano
Forshaw, Peter, 116
Fourier, Charles, 75
Fox, Catherine, 78
Fox, Margaretta, 78 Franck, Adolphe, 77
François 1st, 38
Frater Albertus, see Riedel, Albert Richard
Frederick II, 65
Frederick William II, 65
Freher, Dioysius Andreas, 53
Freitas, Lima de -, 105
Freud, Sigmund, 63, 106
Frick, Karl R. H., 108, 113
Fricker, J. L., 62
Fulcanelli, 90

Gabler, Johann Philipp, 1
Galand, Antoine, 67
Galatino, Pietro, 38
Galvani, Luigi, 69
Ganay, Germain de -, 48
Geber, 30
George of Venice, see Giorgi, Franceso
Georges de Venise, see Giorgi, Franceso
Gichtel, Johann Georg, 42, 43, 51, 73
Gilly, Carlos, 114
Giorgi (or Giorgio), Francesco, 36, 38, 41, 48

Göckel, Rudolf, 62
Godwin, Joscelyn, 108, 112, 113
Goethe, Johann Wolfgang von -, 67, 72, 76, 83
Gohory, Jacques, 47
Goodrick-Clarke, Nicholas, 15, 21, 113, 116
Görres, Joseph von -, 72, 74, 77
Grabianka, Thaddeus Leszczyc, 65
Grasshoff, Carl Louis von -, 85
Gratarolo, Gulielmo, 49
Greenless, Duncan, 91
Grimm, Jakob, 77
Grimm, Wilhelm, 77
Grossato, Alessandro, 113
Grosseteste, see Robert Grosseteste
Guaita, Stanislas de -, 81, 84
Guénon, René, 21, 92, 96–99
Guillaume de Lorris, 33
Gurdjieff, George Ivanovitch, 93, 95, 102, 106, 107
Gutman, Aegidius, 45
Guttierez, Cathy, 17
Guyon (Madame Guyon), see Motte Guyon, J. M. B. de la -

Hahn, Michael, 56
Hahnemann, Samuel, 70
Hakl, Hans Thomas, 116
Hall, Manly Palmer, 105
Hamberger, Julius, 76
Hammer, Olav, 15, 113, 115
Hanegraaff, Wouter J., 13, 16, 17, 112–116
Hardenberg, Friedrich von -, 8, 67, 72
Harris, Frieda, 105
Hartlib, Samuel, 49
Hartmann, Eduard von -, 70

Hartmann, Franz, 81, 84, 87, 88
Hauffe, Friederike, 73
Haugwitz, Christian Heinrich, 66
Haven Marc, see Lalande,
  Emmanuel
Hecht, Koppel, 58
Hegel, Georg W. F., 71
Heindel, Max, see Grasshoff, Carl
  Louis von -
Helmont, Jan Baptista van -, 41
Hepburn, James Bonaventure, 38
Henry, Charles, 81 Heraclitus, 43
Herder, Johann Gottfried, 70
Hermes Trismegistus, 5–6, 25, 37,
  50, 66, 78, 114
Hertum, Cis van -, 114
Hess, Tobias, 44
Hesse, Hermann, 104
Hesteau de Nuysement, Clovis, 49
Hildegard of Bingen, 28
Hippel, F. H. von -, 67
Hitchcock, Ethan Allen, 76
Hochheim, Eckhart von -, 43
Hoffmann, Ernst Theodor Amadeus,
  67, 77
Hohenheim, Theophrastus
  Bombastus von -, 5, 39–41, 43,
  45, 46, 47, 49, 54, 61
Holanda, Francesco, 50
Honoré d'Autun, 28
Honorius Augustodunensis, see
  Honoré d'Autun
Horst, Johann Konrad, 74
Horst, Miers E., 114
Hugo, Victor, 88
Hund, Karl von -, 64
Huser, Johann, 40

Iamblichus, 26

Introvigne, Massimo, 91, 108, 112,
  114

Jacques Coeur, 33
Jean de Meung, 33
Jean Paul, 67
Jennings, Hargrave, 81
Jesus, 78
Joachim da Fiore, 29
John of Sevilla, 30
Jonson, Ben, 51
Joubert, Joseph, 77
Judge, William Quinn, 86
Juncker, Johann, 61
Jung, Carl Gustav, 8, 9, 103, 106,
  107
Jung-Stilling, Johann Heinrich, 57,
  58, 67

Kahn, Didier, 116
Kant, Immanuel, 55, 63, 69
Kardec, Allen, 78
Karl von Hessen-Kassel, 64
Kepler, Johannes, 37, 48
Kerner, Justinus, 72, 73
Khunrath, Heinrich, 41, 43, 49, 50
Kilcher, Andreas, 16
Kirchberger, Niklaus Anton, 57
Kircher, Athanasius, 36, 62, 108
Kichweger, A. J., 54
Kingsford, Anna Bonus, 82, 85, 87,
  101
Knorr von Rosenroth, Christian,
  38, 51
Köppen, Friedrich von -, 66
Kremmerz, Giuliano, 101
Krishna, 78
Krishnamurti, 83
Kristeller, Paul Oskar, 23

Molitor, Franz Joseph, 77
Montfaucon de Villars, 51, 67
Moreau, Gustave, 88
Morin, Jean-Baptiste, 47
Mouravieff, Boris, 93
Moses, 6, 78
Moses of Leon, 31
Motte Guyon, Jeanne Marie Bouvier
   de la -, 54
Mouhy, Charles de Fieux -, 67
Mozart, Wofgang Amadeus, 58, 67
Mylius, D., 50

Nasr, Seyyed Hosseyn, 95, 100
Naxagoras, Ehrd de -, 61
Needleman, Jacob, 114
Neugebauer-Wölk, Monika, 1, 16, 17
Nerval, Gérard de -, 87
Newton, Isaac, 50
Nicholas of Cusa, 29, 36
Nicholas II, 81
Nicolescu, Basarab, 95
Nostradamus, see Michel de Nostre-
   Dame
Novalis, see Hardenberg, Friedrich
   von -, 8, 67, 72
Novikov, Nicolaiy Ivanovich, 64

Oberlin, Jean Frédéric, 57–58
Oersted, Hans Christian, 72
Oetinger, Friedrich Christoph, 55,
   62, 69, 94
Olcott, Henry Steel, 86
Olympiodorus, 26
Origen, 27
Orpheus, 6, 78
Ouspensky, Piotr Dem'ianovich, 81,
   95, 102

Palamidessi, Tomaso, 92

Paley, William, 73
Panteo, Giovanni Agostino, 49
Pantheus, Johannes Antonius, see
   Panteo, Giovanni Agostino
Paolini, Fabio, 48, 51
Papus, see Encausse, Gérard
Paracelsus, see Hohenheim von -,
   Thophrastus Bombastus
Pasi, Marco, 16, 114
Pasqually, see Martines de Pasqually
Patrizi, Francesco, 36
Paul (Saint), 12
Pauwels, Louis, 103
Péladan, Josephin, 81, 84, 88
Pernety, Antoine-Joseph, 61, 65
Pessoa, Fernando, 104
Peter of Abano, see Pietro de
   Abano
Petrus Bonus, 30
Philip the Good, 32
Philip IV the Fair, 64
Philipon, René, 83
Philippe, Anthelme-Nizier, 81
Pico della Mirandola, Giovanni, 37,
   38–40, 107
Pico della Mirandola,
   Gianfrancesco, 6, 49
Pierre d'Ailly, 30
Pietro de Abano, 30
Plato, 6, 23, 39, 61, 78
Plessis-Mornay, Philippe du -, 36
Poeschel, Thomas, 60
Poiret, Pierre, 43, 54
Pordage, John, 43, 73
Porta, Giovanni Batista della -, 46
Portal, Frédéric, 76
Postel, Guillaume, 38, 41
Plotinus, 26, 40
Poe, Edgar Allen, 77
Porphyry, 26

Pouvourville, Albert de -, 96
Prel, Carl du -, 81
Ptolemy, 47
Proclus, 40
Pseudo-Dionysius, *see* Dionysius
Aeropagita
Puységur, A. M. J. de Chastenet
de -, 63
Pythagoras, 1, 6, 59, 78

Rabelais, François, 51
Ragon de Bettignies, Jean-Marie,
75
Raimondo de Sangro di San Severo,
67
Rama, 78
Randolph, Paschal Beverly, 82, 84
Reuchlin, Johannes, 37, 38
Reuss, Theodor, 85
Reynaud, Jean, 75
Richer, Edouard, 75
Richter, Samuel, 54
Ricius, Paulus, 37
Riedel, Albert Richard, 90, 94
Riffard, Pierre, 9, 10, 114
Rijckenborgh, Jan van -, *see* Leene,
Jan
Ripley, George, 31
Ritter, Johann Wilhelm, 72
Rivail, Denizard Hyppolyte Léon,
see Robert de Boron, 33
Robert Grosseteste, 28
Roger of Hereford, 30
Rops, Félicien, 88
Rösler, G. F., 62
Rossel, Hannibal, 36
Roth-Scholtz, Friedrich, 61
Rouault, Georges, 88
Rousse-Lacordaire, Jérôme, 19, 112
Roux, Paul Pierre, 88

Rudhyar, Dane, *see* Chennevière,
Daniel
Rudolf II, 50
Runge, Philipp Otto, 67, 77
Ruyer, Raymond, 96

Saint-Georges de Marsais, Hector
de -, 54
Saint-Germain ('Comte de-'), 59
Saint-Martin, Louis-Claude de -, 56,
57, 60, 64, 67, 71, 72, 74–76,
83, 84
Saint-Pol-Roux, *see* Roux, Paul
Pierre
Saint-Yves d'Alveydre, Joseph
Alexandre, 81, 94
Sallmann, Jean-Michel, 20
Saltzmann, Frédéric-Rodolphe, 56
Sand, George, 76
Santucci, James A., 17, 117
Sarachaga, Alexis de, 85, 86
Satie, Erik, 88
Savalette de Langes, Charles Pierre,
66
Scève, Maurice, 51
Scharfenberg, Albrecht von -, 33
Schaya, Leo, 99
Scheffler, Johann, 51
Scheible, Johann, 78
Schelling, Friedrich W. J. von -,
69, 71
Schlag, Oscar Rudolf, 103, 117
Schlegel, Friedrich, 77
Schneiderfranken, Anton, 105
Scholem, Gershom, 23
Schröder, Friedrich Josef Wilhelm,
61
Schubert, Gotthilf Heinrich von -,
70, 72, 74
Schuon, Frithjof, 99

Schuré, Edouard, 78
Schwartz, Fernand, 102
Schweighart, Theophilus, 45
Scot, Michael, 30
Scott, Cyril, 106
Scotus Eriugena, Johannes, 28, 29
Secret, François, 16
Sédir, Paul, *see* Leloup, Yvon
Servier, Jean, 112
Shakespeare, William, 51, 88
Silberer, Herbert, 106
Sincere Brethern (The -), 27
Sincerus Renatus, *see* Richter,
  Samuel
Smith, Huston, 100
Smith, Pamela Coleman, 105
Solovyov, Vladimir, 83, 92
Spencer, Edmund, 51
Spinoza, Baruch, 69
Starck, Johann August, 66
Steffens, Henrik, 72
Steiner, Rudolf, 8, 83, 85, 87, 88,
  92–94, 101, 105
Stephanos of Alexandria, 26
Stockhausen, Karl Heinz, 106
Stobaeus, 25
Stuckrad, Kocku von -, 16, 115
Studion, Simon, 45
Swedenborg, Emanuel, 55–58, 67,
  75, 76, 94
Synesius, 25

Tasso, *see* Torquato Tasso
Taylor, John, 78
Terrasson, Jean, 58
Thenaud, Jehan 38
Théon, Max, 85
Théot, Catherine, 60
Thomas Aquinas, 29, 30
Thomson, James, 67

Thorndike, Lynn, 23
Tilton, Hereward, 17
Titi, Placido, 47
Tomberg, Valentin, 90, 93
Torquato Tasso, 51
Torreblanca, Francisco, 49
Towianki, André, 75
Tristan, Frederick, 105
Trithemius, Johannes, 46
Troxler, Ignaz, 72
Tschoudy, Théodore Henri de -, 65

Ulstad, Philip, 49

Valentinus, 27
Valin, Georges, 99
Van Eeden, 81
Van Rijnberk, Gérard, 90
Vaughan, Thomas, 49
Versluis, Arthur, 16, 17, 116
Verville, Beroalde de-, 51
Vieillard-Baron, Jean-Louis, 71, 112
Villiers de Lisle-Adam, Auguste
  de -, 88
Vincent de Beauvais, 29
Vismes, Anne Pierre Jacques de -,
  58, 60
Volta, Alessandro, 69
Voss, Karen, 114
Vulliaud, Paul, 81

Wagner, Johann Jacob, 72
Wagner, Richard, 88
Waite, Arthur Edward, 82, 85
Webb, James, 108, 115
Wehr, Gerhard, 8
Weigel, Valentin, 41
Welling, Georg von -, 54
Weor, Samuel Aun, 102
Werner, Zacharias, 67

Westcott, William Winn, 82, 85
Willermoz, Jean-Baptiste, 57, 63, 65
William of Conches, 28
Williams, Charles, 104
Windischmann, Karl Joseph, 59
Woodman, William Robert, 85
Wronski, Hoëné, 75, 89
Wunenburger, Jean-Jacques, 107

Yates, Frances A., 9, 10, 23, 18, 116

Yeats, William Butler, 85

Zetzner, Eberhard, 49
Ziegler, Leopold, 92
Zimmermann, Rolf Christian, 112
Zinnendorf, Johann Wilhelm, 65
Zoroaster, 6
Zorzi, *see* Giorgi, Francesco
Zozimus of Panapolis, 26